Does
Your
Government **?**
Measure Up **?**

Does Your Government Measure Up?

♦ ♦ ♦

Basic Tools for Local Officials and Citizens

William D. Coplin & Carol Dwyer

Syracuse University   Syracuse, New York

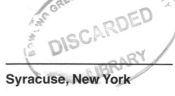

First Edition 2000
00 01 02 03 04 05 06 07   7 6 5 4 3 2 1

The paper used in this publication meets the minimum requirements
of American National Standard for Information Sciences – Permanence
of Paper for Printed Library Materials, ANSI Z39.48-1984. ∞™

Library of Congress Cataloging-in-Publication Data
available upon request from the authors
William D. Coplin and Carol Dwyer
ISBN 0-9702864-0-6

Manufactured in the United States of America

Contents

Acknowledgments

This book has truly been a collaborative effort. Our colleagues at the Maxwell School and the Alfred P. Sloan, Jr. Foundation as well as many local municipal officials and more than 75 talented undergraduate students have played a major part in shaping this book. The following individuals have played a special role. Ted Greenwood, program officer with the Alfred P. Sloan Foundation, has supported the Maxwell School's Community Benchmarks Program from the beginning through his thoughtful insight. Friend and colleague Astrid Merget has encouraged our writing of this book while sharing her wisdom and experience. Jeffrey Stonecash provided advice for the entire book and drafted the appendix on surveys. S. Trevor Bowen performed a first rate job of designing a reader-friendly book. Ashley Walter was an essential participant in making overall improvements. Tiffany Blair and Jessica White spent many hours conducting research and reviews in the early stages. Renee Gadua and Barbara Decker provided outstanding copy editing and rewriting services. Michelle Walker was the catalyst for an eleventh hour title change. Angela Ward has taken care of a myriad of details and constantly tries to keep us organized.

Several current and former municipal officials provided crucial reality checks to assure that our material was clear and relevant. Early input was given by Robert Bird, Clyde Ohl and Frank Wilson. Salient reviews were provided by Vincent Palerino, Kevin Holmquist, Kathleen Rapp, Miles Ross and Karen Shultz. Judith Mower and Charlotte Holstein of Forging Our Community's United Strengths (FOCUS of Greater Syracuse) provided us with a forum of local leaders who gave us a reality check. They include Russ Andrews, Mary Ann Coogan, Lorene Dadey, Patrick DiDomenico, James Hotchkiss, Julia Kanaley, Frances Kip, Minch Lewis, Sherry Mossotti, Kathleen O'Hara, Bill Pavlus, Dennis Pelmear, William Sanford and Michael Walsh.

We also wish to thank the functional experts who contributed suggestions for our checklists, they include Meredith Hellestrae of the Commission on Accreditation of Ambulance Services, Bill Hartz of Building Officials Code Administrators International, Dr. Betty van der Smissen of the American Parks & Recreation Society, Dennis Ross of American Public Works Association, Peg Gant of the Commission on Accreditation for Law Enforcement Agencies, Annie Aubrey of the Association of International Assessing Officers, Richard DeGroot of DeGroot Management Services, Bert Waisanen of the Government Finance Officers Association and Kristen Cormier-Robinson of the Council of State Governments.

Introduction

We have written this book in the belief that local governments could be greatly improved if officials and citizens consistently ask a simple question: *Does my government measure up?* This question clearly evokes the idea of continuous improvement and carries with it a commitment to collect information on a systematic basis and to track progress. Measurement defines continuous improvement in the business world where the phrase is viewed as the key to success. We believe that government and citizens can reap the same benefits.

This book has two fundamental approaches to help you find the answer to whether *your government measures up*. The first and most basic is to apply a checklist of the *bare essentials* to local government operations, such as assessment, building codes and finance. *Bare essential* checklists and follow up information are provided in Part One. The second approach is to use *benchmarking*, a term first developed in the business world to improve operations. Part Two provides a primer on how benchmarking will help you assess your government.

These two simple ideas – a checklist for minimum government standards and benchmarking to assess efficiency and effectiveness – can be used by:

◆ Elected officials to monitor government managers
◆ Government managers to perform self-checks
◆ Political candidates who support government accountability
◆ Citizens to keep the politicians on track

We are convinced by our experience with elected officials in the towns and villages of Central New York that this book can make a difference.

We are not naïve about how easily people will embrace the checklist and benchmarking process. An elected official in a medium sized town near a highly urbanized area wrote the following after reviewing a draft of this book:

> *From being in the political world and seeing how things are done, the draft is unrealistic... We had a situation where one of the board members decided to study the costs of a government service through a careful study. When the public found out about the study, the board member lost the next election even though the study would have helped save money and improve the service...*

Everything is kept very hush-hush… If things don't need to be out there for the public to see, it won't be unless requested.

Most board members work fulltime and we rely on a fulltime manager to virtually run the township… We don't meet that often – only once or twice a month for regular business and then when things demand such as budgets, personnel, etc.

These remarks show the forces that deter this government official from asking the questions necessary to answer how well his government measures up. We believe that this book will be a powerful tool to those of us who would like to see improved performance and greater accountability in government. We hope that readers will at least try some of the checklists and benchmarking procedures to start the process.

Part One

Checking for Bare Essentials

*I always wanted to be somebody,
but I should have been more specific.*

Lily Tomlin, *Comedian*

*Check the vital signs of your local
government with a list of minimum
standards for your local government.
Chapter One introduces our checklists.
The remaining chapters offer specific checklists
for eight areas of local government,
as well as municipal Web sites.*

Chapter 1

The Importance of Checking for Bare Essentials

Learn About

✓ **The usefulness of checklists**
✓ **Bare necessities of good government**
✓ **Customer surveys**
✓ **Accreditation**

Checklists are a way of getting specific. Using our checklist of bare essentials for good government is like assessing vital signs and conducting the initial blood work your doctor requires as part of your physical examination. It will help identify trouble spots that need further investigation.

The nine chapters that follow each provide five to 10 bare essentials that have been carefully selected on the advice of professionals who advise government officials. They are the minimum standards for good local government. They are a partial list of those we think you can apply without technical training and time-consuming work. Those interested in going to the next level should read the "beyond bare essentials" section found in each chapter.

Don't Be Surprised

Although we have listed only the minimum requirements, you should not be surprised to learn that your local government does not follow some basic recommended practices.

For example, one of the first standards identified in the Government Finance section lists that an annual independent audit be conducted.

While most local governments are multimillion dollar businesses, they all do not meet this requirement. That is why we started this book with what we consider the first level – a basic checklist for eight operational areas. You can go through the list with the respective department heads or other appropriate officials to quickly evaluate your municipality. Each municipality should have a check by every one of these standards. If not, corrective action needs to occur.

It is best to ask for confirmation that the standard has been reached. If the comptroller says an audit has been conducted, then ask to see the latest report. If the law enforcement agency in your community says it has a procedure for handling complaints, ask for a copy of the guidelines. If the commissioner of the department of public works says there are written goals for training within each job classification, you should ask to see what is written and then ask how the training matches up with the goals. If your municipality has an employee handbook, when was the last time it was updated?

You may also find that what appears to be an obvious suggestion can stir up serious conflict. For example, suggesting that the assessment department implement a customer survey either at the point of service delivery, or via mail or telephone, can meet with serious opposition.

Resistance from the office staff may occur for at least three reasons:

- ◆ They already have enough to do
- ◆ Survey results may feed into their performance reviews
- ◆ In some offices, such as property assessment, citizens are perceived as being irritated before they walk through the door.

All of these reasons may be legitimate, but they can be addressed through careful survey design, employee education about the process and, most important, experiencing the results. We have been told by elected officials that customer surveys are unnecessary because *elections are the only survey I need.* Officials in municipalities where one political party is dominant and a challenger seldom emerges usually espouse this philosophy. The voting history in many communities indicates a large number of citizens eligible to vote, do not, which means re-election is seldom indicative of a ground swell of support. Refusal to give consideration to any form of customer survey should send a message to citizens and government employees that continuous improvement is not valued.

Customer Surveys as a Key Bare Essential

While we are on the subject of customer surveys, you will note that feedback between governments and citizens is called for in eight of the nine areas discussed in this section. Arthur Andersen, one of the world's leading consulting companies, cites customer-focused solutions[1] as being the linchpin of continuous improvement in a study of best practices. The Customer Survey Success Story below illustrates how this holds true for government services.

A Customer Survey Success Story

In upstate New York, Carolee A. Conklin became the Rochester City Clerk in 1994. The city merged the offices of clerk and treasurer into one unit under Conklin. This expanded role meant that her office was two floors away from most of her staff. In 1995, Conklin began using customer surveys to help manage her new responsibilities. Every person who completes the survey and includes their name and address receives a letter thanking them. Although form letters are used, both Conklin and the city council president hand-sign the letters. If a survey response is negative, the deputy clerk immediately contacts the person. Based on customer feedback, several operational changes have resulted, such as the clarification of written and voice instructions. Admitting that employees were initially wary of the surveys, Conklin contends that they have had a positive effect.[2] A survey that specifically mentions an employee by name, either in praise or criticism, is placed in the personnel file and communicated to the worker. Convinced that the customer surveys have been a catalyst for continuous improvement, Conklin says the office has enjoyed an approval rating of over 94 percent over each of the five years surveys have been used. "I believe we really are here to serve the public," says Conklin, who gives copies of the annual reports on the survey results to city councilors and staff.

The value of an established customer service survey procedure has been confirmed in our work with many local government units. We have been asked on a regular basis to develop simple customer survey instruments for a variety of areas.

Just the use of customer surveys in a department creates a different relationship between government employees and the public, which can result in better service and cost-savings. The department clearly

---

[1] Hiebeler, Robert, Thomas B. Kelly and Charles Ketteman. *Best Practices: Building Your Business with Customer-Focused Solutions.* New York: Simon and Schuster. 1998.

[2] Based on telephone interviews conducted by Carol Dwyer with Carolee Conklin on June 12, 1998, and June 15, 2000.

communicates to everyone that the continuous improvement is important and that government personnel and citizens need to work together.

Given the potential impact that customer surveys can have, we consider them to be one of the most important activities a government can undertake to improve efficiency and effectiveness in service areas.

Beyond Bare Essentials

The bare essential checklist is only the beginning of the process of developing a continuous improvement approach to government services. As problems are addressed and solutions are explored, new ideas emerge that might lead to new job definitions, redefined missions, lower costs and more employee and customer satisfaction.

Some of the items in the checklist require a complex set of activities. An independent audit by a professional accountant or developing a general security plan for local parks may require operational changes. An inability to follow the recommended practices may indicate a serious lack of institutional capacity to perform the job that is required.

Applying our bare essential checklist is the first step in bringing higher levels of performance to government agencies. If the checklist reveals problems, a more elaborate self-assessment procedure is in order. This process can be greatly aided by the professional associations that have helped us create the checklists. Use the information in the chapter to explore a list of standards beyond the checklist we have provided. Contact these and other agencies for publications, training and consulting if you are seriously concerned. The associations review best practices and are able to provide guidance to continuously improve your government.

The ultimate level of continuous improvement that logically develops from our checklist is the application of standards through accreditation. Some governments sponsor formal accreditation programs. For example, the New York State Association of Chiefs of Police works in cooperation with the New York State Sheriffs Association and the New York State Division of Criminal Justice Services to accredit law enforcement agencies in the state. The New York State Law Enforcement Accreditation Program uses 149 standards and goals. In Onondaga County, 10 out of 16 police departments have this accreditation.

National accreditation can be expensive, and compliance may be labor intensive. To get an idea of the procedure and costs, take a look at the box on the next page, which lists the eight steps of the Commission for

Accreditation of Park and Recreation Agencies (CAPRA). Your government may choose not to undertake such a significant allocation of resources, but as technology and society become increasingly complex, accreditation will become more common. Lower insurance liability costs may offset the accreditation costs.

Whether or not using the checklists provided in the next nine chapters leads to serious cooperation with one of the professional associations, asking the specific questions in our checklist will help you learn how committed your government is to the idea of continuous improvement. Once that idea takes hold, progress is inevitable. Applying the checklist is a way of making specific improvements and changing the culture of the government.

Commission for Accreditation of Park and Recreation Agencies Process

Step 1. Preliminary Application

A preliminary application and fee notify the commission of the department's interest and initial investment. It is recommended that the person in the department coordinating the self-assessment process attend a Visitor Training Workshop to get insights into the various standards and evidence for compliance. The workshop registration fee is included in the preliminary application fee.

Step 2. Self-Assessment

The department's own self assessment is the major element of the process which may take up to a year to complete. The self-assessment results in a comprehensive written report documenting each applicable standard. The department reaps great benefit from the self-assessment process, whether or not the department chooses to continue with accreditation. A self-assessment workbook (a computer disk) is available to assist a department in preparing the self assessment report.

Step 3. Formal Application:

The formal application is submitted with the department's self assessment and indicates the department's commitment to the on-site review process and to paying costs associated with initial and continuing accreditation. The application is accompanied by a fee and indicates dates for an on-site review. Costs: the department pays a preliminary fee of $100 (Step 1). A fee paid at the time of formal application (Step 3) and the annual maintenance fee (Step 8) are based on a sliding scale according to the size of the department's operation budget for traditional park and recreation functions (for scale, see publication An Overview...).

Step 4: Site Visit/Review.

A site visitation team of peers spends 2-3 days at the department, reviewing written documentation, interviewing staff, board members, and users at all levels, and visiting department facilities, to verify the self assessment. The visitors are experienced park and recreation professionals from similar departments who have applied to the commission to serve in this capacity and have received substantial visitor training.

Step 5: Report

The team prepares a written report to the commission detailing its findings, standard by standard, and indicating whether in its judgement the standard was met and if not, what was lacking. The department has opportunity to review the visitation team report and is invited to provide a written response to the commission.

Step 6: Commission Review

A review before the commission culminates the process, bringing together commission members, department representatives and the chair of the site review team to assess all documentation and make the final decision to accredit or not to accredit. Few departments who have made the effort to reach this point will "fail", though the commission may require compliance with specified conditions by a specific date in order to be accredited.

Step 7: Publicity

Publicizing the department's achievement is important to the department and its municipality, to the commission and to the profession. The commission will assist in such promotion.

Step 8: Accreditation Maintenance.

To maintain accreditation, departments must pay an annual maintenance fee and submit an update report to the commission. Departments must apply to renew full accreditation every five years and performance goals are set based on those practices.

Main Points

✓ **Start with your government checklist.**

✓ **Determine if your government meets the bare essentials test.**

✓ **Quality assurance is important.**

✓ **Professional associations raise the bar for government operations.**

Chapter 2

Ambulance Services

Learn About

✓ **Basic functions of ambulance services**
✓ **The Commission on Accreditation of Ambulance Services**
✓ **Checklist for ambulance services**

Emergency medical services (EMS) is the provision of medical care during an emergency, encompassing on-scene and transport medical care, 911-call screening, call dispatch, public education, vehicle maintenance and hospital facilities. Emergency Medical Technicians (EMTs), paramedics and trauma specialists provide competent care during rescue and transport to hospitals.

Millions of Americans require emergency care and pre-hospital transport each year. In providing these services, minutes count as well as the level of EMS medical training and the sophistication of the medical equipment. These factors, among others, can make a difference in life or death outcomes.

Projected future trends include:

◆ Increase in community-based services such as home visits and immunizations.

◆ Aggressive education programs emphasizing prevention.

◆ Greater numbers of fire departments providing EMS as well as partnerships with private services.

◆ New technology to expand the level of care available from EMS providers.

This chapter is based on material provided by The Commission on Accreditation of Ambulance Services (CAAS).

- Increased need for EMS due to heightened risk of terrorism and violent acts.
- More need for EMS with an aging population.
- Economic uncertainty because of the negative impacts from rising HMO, Medicare and other healthcare costs.

In the face of many new challenges, EMS providers will need to be extremely well-run, community-integrated agencies. Communities that support and demand quality care will need recognized quality standards for their EMS services.

Key Sources

The Commission on Accreditation of Ambulance Services (CAAS), an independent accrediting agency, was established to encourage and promote the highest standards for medical transport systems. The CAAS accreditation is open to services of all types: public, private, fire-based, inter-facility, volunteer or hospital-based. Its nine-member board of directors represents six leading national EMS organizations: The American Ambulance Association, the Emergency Nurses Association, the International Association of Fire Chiefs, the National Association of EMS Physicians, the National Association of EMTs and the National Association of State EMS Directors.

Most states and many local governments have regulatory requirements for ambulance operations. Many professional associations, EMS experts and government standards were used to build the CAAS standards. For more information regarding the CAAS accreditation process, contact the Commission by phone, fax, or e-mail, or visit the CAAS Web site.

Contact Information

**The Commission on Accreditation
of Ambulance Services (CAAS)**

David L. Stumph
Executive Director
Email: daves@tcag.com

Meredith Hellestrae
Administrator
Email:meredithh@tcag.com

1926 Waukegan Rd, Suite 1
Glenview, IL 60025

www.caas.org

847-657-6828
Fax: 657-6825

Bare Essentials

1. Develop a preplanned written process for mutual aid.

The agency should have a preplanned written process for dealing with mutual aid needs and requests. The existence of a comprehensive disaster plan is important to ensure that the community is protected from unpredictable incidents that may tax the existing infrastructure.

2. Maintain a continuous education program.

The agency shall have a Continuing Medical Education program that meets or exceeds local and state requirements with physician approval. The Continuing Medical Education program shall be clearly linked to the agency's Continuous Quality Improvement (CQI) Program.

3. Develop clearly stated response time standards.

The agency shall have established standards for (1) total time to process a request prior to it being assigned to an ambulance; (2) total time for an ambulance to start responding once notified of a request; (3) total response time (defined as the difference in time from the point where the location of the patient, the callback number, and the problem type are known if possible until the time when an appropriate responding crew advises that they have arrived at the scene). These time intervals will be defined for life-threatening, emergency and non-emergency requests. Differences in response time standards by geographic area will be described. In life-threatening requests, the total response time standard will be eight minutes and 59 seconds, or less, 90 percent of the time; unless the medical director has determined that this standard is not feasible due to uncontrollable circumstances (such as in very rural settings). Response time standards are to be set by administration, in conjunction with the medical director. Any established state/local response time standards will be used as a minimum standard.

4. Ensure medical oversight by a licensed physician.

The agency shall have a duly licensed physician, or physicians, responsible for medical oversight. Responsibilities shall include, at a minimum: development and authorization of clinical dispatch, patient care, and transport protocols; advisory and approval role in training/education of medical employees; advisory and approval role in clinical CQI initiatives; and advisory and approval role in EMS System design.

5. Develop a contingency plan for backup of equipment and power.

The Communications Center shall have a contingency plan to provide immediate backup communications equipment and/or power source to continue operation in the event of equipment or power failure. The contingency plan shall have, at a minimum, two levels of backup.

Beyond Bare Essentials

The current CAAS Standards are divided into 10 sections and subdivided into 55 standard areas. Within the standards, 140 characteristics require agency compliance. An EMS agency wanting to be CAAS-accredited must meet or be in full compliance with every characteristic of the standards for each category listed below:

Organization

- Ownership
- Organizational Structure
- Management

Inter-Agency Relations

- Mutual Aid
- Disaster Coordination
- Conflict Resolution
- Interagency Dialogue

Management

- Documentation
- Policies and Procedures
- Planning
- Safety
- Management Development

Financial Management

- Financial Policy
- Budget
- Financial Statements
- Billing and Collections

Community Relations and Public Information

- Community Education
- Community Relations
- Media Relations

Personnel and the Personnel Process

- Job Descriptions
- Credentials
- Compensation
- Nondiscrimination
- Grievances
- Discipline
- Recruitment
- Orientation/Training
- Performance Appraisals
- Minimum Qualifications
- Professional Conduct

Clinical Standards

- Existence of Protocols
- Adherence to Protocols
- Personnel Qualifications
- Continuing Education
- Response Times
- Quality Assurance
- Staffing

Other Standards of Operation

- Safety Restraints
- Patient Property
- Incident Reporting Process
- Driver Training/Vehicle Operations
- Loss Control

Equipment and Facilities

- Ambulance Vehicles
- Medical Equipment
- Disposable Items
- Care & Maintenance of Reusable Items
- Preventive Maintenance
- Daily Checklists
- Facilities

Other Standards of Operation

- Written Procedures
- Time Records
- Dispatcher Training
- Preventive Maintenance
- Contingency Plan
- Licensure

Quick Checklist for Ambulance Services

❑ Develop a preplanned written process for mutual aid.

❑ Maintain a continuous education program.

❑ Develop clearly stated response time standards.

❑ Ensure medical oversight by a licensed physician.

❑ Develop a contingency plan for backup of equipment and power.

Chapter 3

Building Code Enforcement

Learn About

✓ **The advantages of enforcing building codes**
✓ **Where to go for more information**
✓ **Checklist for building code enforcement**

We all need protection from tragedy caused by fire, structural collapse and general deterioration in our homes, schools, stores and manufacturing facilities. Building codes provide protection by reducing potential hazards to building occupants.

Building safety is achieved through proper design and construction practices and a code administration program that ensures compliance. Poor code enforcement jeopardizes investments made in homes and businesses.

Building codes provide uniformity in the construction industry. In addition, they establish predictable and consistent minimum standards, which are applied to the quality and durability of construction materials, a practical balance between reasonable safety and cost to protect life and property. This means that effective code enforcement meets the criteria of being both practical and adequate for protecting the life, safety and welfare of the public.

Performing inspections during construction is the only way to verify that code compliance has been achieved. On average, 10 inspections are conducted in homes, offices or factories to verify conformity to minimum standards.

This chapter is based on materials provided by William Hartz of Building Officials and Code Administrators, International (BOCA).

Finally, effective building code enforcement contributes to the well-being of the community. The preservation of life and safety, as well as the maintenance of property values over time, are a direct result of the application and enforcement of model building codes. In addition to safety, building codes encourage the intelligent use of energy resources that will save money.

Key Sources

Code enforcement underwent a dramatic change in the late 1990s. Beginning in the year 2000, one set of construction code documents will be supported and eventually used throughout the entire nation. The International Codes are a family of codes that include building, plumbing, mechanical, fire, property maintenance, energy conservation, and zoning. These documents are supported by the nation's three major Model Code Organizations.

Protection of the public through effective code enforcement is not hard to achieve. Unfortunately, code enforcement with inadequate codes and untrained staff will cost just as much but will not provide the benefits.

To get detailed information about how the codes are developed, purchasing the codes, certification of code officials or even starting a code enforcement office you may contact one of these organizations:

Contact Information

International Code Council (ICC)
5203 Leesburg Pike, Suite 708
Falls Church, VA 22041-3401
703-931-4533
www.intlcode.org

**Building Officials and
Code Administrators
International, Inc. (BOCA)**
4051 West Flossmoor Drive
Country Club Hills, IL 60478-5795
800-214 4321
www.bocai.org

**International Conference
of Building Officials (ICBO)**
5360 Workman Mill Road
Whittier, CA 90601-2298
800-284-4406
www.icbo.org

**Southern Building Code
Congress International, Inc.
(SBCCI)**
900 Montclair Road
Birmingham, AL 35213-1206
205-591-1853
www.sbcci.org

Bare Essentials

1. Clearly indicate the source of the standards used.

Many states have adopted a statewide construction code. If that is the case in your state, check with the appropriate state agency to determine what codes must be enforced. If code adoption is a local decision, you will face the decision of what code to adopt. There are many older editions of the model codes, state written codes and even codes written by local jurisdictions. At best these will be outdated.

The model code organizations listed on the previous page support one set of code documents for the entire nation – The International Codes. This means that all inspectors, plan examiners, code officials, architects, engineers, building contractors and manufacturers will be working with a consistent set of requirements in the United States.

Depending on your state and the history of your office, the standards used may not be from The International Codes. Over the long run, your code enforcement office should be encouraged to adopt The International Codes. However the office should be able to tell you what codes they are using, their source and their date of development.

2. Obtain membership in a model code organization.

Why? You will need support. Model code organizations offer technical support, training, credentialing programs plus membership prices on their products. For example, members can call their BOCA office daily to receive verbal or written code interpretations, to discuss administrative issues or to find out about new construction materials from BOCA's Evaluation Services Department. New Jersey and Virginia officials feel membership in a model code organization is so important that they provide every jurisdiction in their state with BOCA membership. Contact the model code organization of your choice to discuss the advantages of membership.

3. Seek certification of inspectors and plan reviewers.

It is important that the people you hire to enforce the code are experienced and knowledgeable about the codes. All of the model code organizations offer certification programs. Many state programs require certification of the code official. The certification means that the individual is knowledgeable about the codes.

The certification programs are based on a series of examinations that measure the person's ability to use and understand the codes. Certifications are available in all disciplines of code enforcement: accessibility, building, plumbing, mechanical, electrical, fire, energy, property maintenance and zoning. A certification program will assure the communities served of the validity of services they receive and will assist in ensuring more uniform code enforcement.

It is important that you also interview the individual to be sure he meets the requirements of your community concerning service, working with people and dedication to the community.

Qualified code professionals are key to the success of your code enforcement program.

4. Support training programs for technical employees with adequate annual funding.

Continuing education is important because new editions of codes are issued every three years. Code officials and support staff should also stay current with changing technology. Each of the model code organizations offers training programs for entry level to the most advanced positions.

If your state has adopted a statewide code enforcement program, the state may require continuing education to renew certification. It is important that officials in each jurisdiction support their code officials in the area of continuing education.

5. Develop affordable and easily understood appeals process.

The appeals process should be detailed clearly and concisely in a document distributed to people considering an appeal. The cost of filing an appeal should be minimal, optimally no more than the actual cost.

Often the level of code enforcement can be determined by the ability to appeal a code official's decision. Building designers, property owners, or contractors must know that there is a fair and impartial way to disagree with a code official's decision. Your jurisdiction should have several qualified individuals willing to serve on an appeals board. Establishment of an appeals board is outlined by code organizations or may be established through state laws.

6. Ensure sufficient staffing to meet the demand for inspections.

Consider two guidelines. First, new construction inspections should be conducted within three days of a request, unless state or local laws require a shorter time period. Second, inspectors should not be required to conduct more than an average of 10 inspections per day. These guidelines are a minimum standard. Failure to meet these guidelines on a regular basis may mean a jurisdiction should consider whether additional staff may be necessary.

These checklist items help you conduct an initial scan of the operation of your code enforcement office. You can conduct a more thorough analysis based on the guidelines that follow. You may also want to consider using an outside consultant to conduct a systematic audit and issue a report that will provide additional information.

Beyond Bare Essentials

Codes and Standards

♦ *Are the codes current and widely accepted?* Using outdated or regional codes often leads to confusion among building designers, owners and contractors and may result in more expensive construction that is passed on to the consumer. The codes you are following should be based on state or international codes and they should be updated on a regular basis, minimally every three years.

♦ *Are copies available for the public?* Homeowners often need a reference to understand the code. A well-run code office provides a copy of the codes for public use. You may also consider having copies available at the local library.

Code Enforcement Office

♦ *Are the business hours convenient to the contractors and the public?* In small jurisdictions, the code office may not be open every day or all day, but the hours should be posted. Every jurisdiction should consider keeping the code office open at least one evening a week. This should be expanded to reflect volume.

♦ *Is the support staff knowledgeable and friendly?* Knowledge and service are the keys to success. If the code official is doing inspections, someone should be available to accept plans, discuss fees and explain the reason a permit is required. Any process that requires additional steps should be outlined in a one-page handout that users can follow.

Plan Examination

♦ *Are plans required and reviewed before construction?* Plan review is essential. It is much easier to erase a pencil mark than to tear down a wall. The code official must be able to interpret blueprints and be sufficiently familiar with the codes so that mistakes can be detected.

♦ *Are plans modified before construction?* If mistakes are found, a system should be in place that provides for the submittal of corrections.

Office Management

♦ *Are plans stored for the life of the structure?* Considering the current technology, considerable space can be conserved by archiving computerized plans. However, paper is still the norm in many jurisdictions.

♦ *Are thorough records maintained that can be easily accessed?* A file should be created for each property as work is completed. This will create a construction history for every property. The filing system is often based on the street address, parcel number or block and lot. Many computer-based permit application packages are available for office management and record collection. A system also needs to be in place to report all construction information to the tax office.

- *Are your fees sufficient to maintain the code office?* Fees should cover the cost of staff, vehicles, office space, and any other related expenditures.
- *Is your technical inspection staff qualified?* The success of any office is based on the ability of the staff.
- *Is the value code enforcement communicated to your community?* It is important that the people you serve know the value of this service.

Quick Checklist for Building Code Enforcement

❑ Clearly indicate the source of the standards used.

❑ Obtain membership in a model code organization.

❑ Seek certification of inspectors and plan reviewers.

❑ Support training programs for technical employees with adequate annual funding.

❑ Develop affordable and easily understood appeals process.

❑ Ensure sufficient staffing to meet the demand for inspections.

Chapter 4

Government Finance

Learn About

✓ **The central role of government finance**
✓ **Sources of standards to assess management of government finances**
✓ **Checklist for the management of government finances**

The fiscal situation confronting local, state, and federal governments in the past decade has made it increasingly difficult for elected officials to balance the requirements of sound financial management and citizen demand for increased service. Officials need to be able to identify needs in the community, rank these needs and allocate the correct amount of funding. The following information can help elected officials to better allocate the scarce financial resources.

The professional management of government financial resources is one of the most, if not the most, important requirement for good local government. There is no quicker way for an elected government official to lose credibility than to be accused of mismanaging the taxpayers' money. Even if mismanagement is not the issue, clarity in providing information and an openness to public scrutiny are key to maintaining public support.

This chapter is based on materials provided by the Government Finance Officer Association (GFOA).

Key Sources

Several organizations provide information on performance standards for the management of government financial resources. The information in this chapter is provided by the Government Finance Officers Association (GFOA). *Recommended Practices for State and Local Governments* provides a clear and comprehensive introduction to the standards in the field.

The association also provides training, certification of finance officers and consultation.

Other publications by the GFOA that may be helpful:

+ *An Elected Official's Guide to Fund Balance*, Stephen J. Gauthier, GFOA, 1989.
+ *An Elected Official's Guide to Auditing*, Stephen J. Gauthier, GFOA, 1992.
+ *An Elected Official's Guide to Internal Controls and Fraud Prevention*, Stephen J. Gauthier, GFOA, 1994.
+ *An Elected Official's Guide to Financial Reporting*, Stephen J. Gauthier, GFOA, 1995.
+ *An Elected Official's Guide to Investing,* M. Corrine Larson, GFOA, 1995.
+ *A Guide to Preparing a Debt Policy*, Patricia Tigue, GFOA, 1998.

Another organization that provides standards in the field is the Government Accounting Standards Board (GASB). The GASB was organized to establish standards for financial accounting and reporting for local and state government agencies. Standards determined by the GASB are used to aid in the preparation of financial reports for these agencies.

Contact Information

Government Accounting Standards Board (GASB)	Government Finance Officers Association (GFOA)
401 Merritt 7, PO Box 5116	180 N Michigan Ave.
Norwalk, CT 06856	Chicago, IL 60601
www.gasb.org	www.gfoa.org
203-847-0700	312-977-9700
Fax: 849-9714	

Bare Essentials

1. Conduct an annual independent audit.

Government agencies obtain an annual independent audit of their financial statements performed in accordance with generally accepted accounting principles and standards.

2. Make finance reports public within six months.

A public report should be issued on a timely basis, no later than six months after the close of the fiscal year, so that the information is relevant.

3. Maintain an inventory of fixed assets.

A physical inventory of capitalized fixed assets, either simultaneously or on a rotating basis, should be conducted at least every five years.

4. Store computer disaster recovery policies off-site.

A copy of the government's formal computer disaster recovery policies with procedures kept off-site to ensure their availability in the event of a disaster.

5. Use competitive bidding for banking services.

Periodically initiate competitive bidding and negotiation processes, in accordance with state and local laws and regulations, for major banking services. The processes should include requests for proposals and should cover services, fees, earnings, credit rates and availability schedules for deposited funds.

6. Make budget summary available.

Provide a concise budget summary. This summary should articulate priorities and key issues for the new budget period, summarize major financial factors and trends, as well as provide data on revenues, other resources and expenditures for a three-year period (prior, current and proposed year). The summary should indicate if the budget is balanced. If not, provide an explanation.

7. Adopt a policy covering charges and fees.

A formal policy regarding charges and fees should be adopted and publicized. The policy should identify which factors are to be taken into account when pricing goods and services. The policy should state whether the jurisdiction intends to recover the full cost of providing goods and services. It also should set forth under what circumstances the jurisdiction might set a charge or fee at more or less than 100 percent of full cost. If the full cost of a good or service is not recovered, the policy should provide the government's rationale for this deviation.

Beyond Bare Essentials

In addition to the standards presented, the GFOA identifies many more standards. The items below are selected from the GFOA book, *Recommended Practices for State and Local Governments.*

Accounting, Auditing, and Financial Reporting Recommended Practices

- Governmental Accounting, Auditing and Financial Reporting Practices
- Preparing Popular Reports
- Audit Procurement

Budgeting and Financial Management Recommended Practices

- Economic Development Incentives
- Performance Measures
- Providing a Concise Summary of the Budget

Retirement of Benefits Administration Recommended Practices

- Public Employee Retirement Investments
- Funding of Public Employee Retirement Systems
- Employee Involvement in Health Plan Changes
- Encouraging Financial and Retirement Planning
- Public Pension Plan Design Consideration

Debt Management Recommended Practices

- Securitization of Leases
- Selecting and Managing the Method of Sale of State and Local Government Bonds
- Analyzing Debt Capacity and Establishing Debt Limits
- Investment of Bond Proceeds
- Securitization of Tax-Exempt Bonds

Cash Management Recommended Practices

- Collateralization of Public Deposits
- Use of Various Types of Mutual Funds by Public Cash Managers
- Selection of Investment Advisers
- Same-day Funds Settlement Procedures
- Diversification of Investments in Portfolio
- Procurement of Banking Services
- Purchasing Card Programs
- Check Fraud Protection

Quick Checklist for Government Finance

❏ **Conduct an annual independent audit.**

❏ **Make finance reports public within six months.**

❏ **Maintain an inventory of fixed assets.**

❏ **Store computer disaster recovery policies off-site.**

❏ **Use competitive bidding for banking services.**

❏ **Make budget summary available.**

❏ **Adopt a policy covering charges and fees.**

Chapter 5

Human Resources

Learn About

✓ Basic functions of human resources
✓ Support from professional associations
✓ Checklist for human resources

A municipality is as good as the people working for it. Personnel policies play a crucial role in the sound operation of local government. Whether or not a formal personnel or human resource (HR) department exists in your government, some administrative operations must occur to ensure a productive work force, legal compliance and employee satisfaction. Such operations are critical to:

- Select and recruit competent employees
- Classify and compensate employees on an equitable basis
- Improve the efficiency and effectiveness of the work force
- Train workers for ever-changing jobs
- Comply with federal, state and local laws
- Avoid lawsuits over an increasing variety of work force issues
- Deal with individual employee issues on a consistent and fair basis

Key Sources

Many professional associations provide services and advice that can improve the work of local government. Some are targeted at specific functional areas and training specific local officials. However, we recommend that you look at a variety of organizations that can help you assess the personnel policies of your government.

This chapter is based on materials provided by the Management Assistance Program for Nonprofits (MAP) and DeGroot Management, Inc.

Two sources were used to develop this chapter's checklist of bare essentials. The first is information provided by Carter McNamara, Ph.D. of the Management Assistance Program for Nonprofits (MAP) in St. Paul, Minnesota. While the information found on MAP's Web site is targeted to nonprofit organizations, many of the categories contain recommendations that can be universally used by governments and businesses as well as nonprofits. The second source is national consultant David DeGroot of DeGroot Management, Inc. Contact information is provided for both.

Additional potential sources include national associations or their state affiliates such as the Conference of Mayors, Association of Towns and the Association of Counties. Contact information for these and other national organizations can be found at the back of the book. The International Personnel Management Association (IPMA) does not provide measurable standards, but the organization offers professional development programs, training opportunities, research services and numerous publications designed to assist human resource managers at all levels.

Contact Information

**International
Personnel Management
Association (IPMA)**
www.ipma-hr.org
703-549-7100

**DeGroot Management
Services, Inc.**
PO Box 502
Syracuse, NY 13213
800-295-6666
Fax: 315-637-0299

**The Management Assistance
Program (MAP) for Nonprofits**
2233 University Avenue West
Suite 360
St. Paul, MN 55114-1629
651-647-1216
Fax: 647-1369
www.mapnp.org

Bare Essentials

1. Develop a personnel policy handbook.

The handbook must be reviewed regularly and updated. It should describe policies for recruitment, hiring, termination, retirement, vacation time, sick and personal days, other fringe benefits, salary schedule, incentive system, staff development and standard work rules for all staff. All policies need to maintain compliance with government regulations, including the Fair Labor Standards Act, Equal Employment Opportunity Act, Americans with Disabilities Act, Occupational Health and Safety Act, Family Leave Act and Affirmative Action Plan.

Copies of the handbook must be available to all staff and members of the board. Staff members should acknowledge in writing that they have read and have access to the personnel handbook/policies.

2. Develop job descriptions for all positions.

Be certain to include qualifications, duties, reporting relationships and key indicators in all job descriptions.

3. Conduct employee performance appraisals.

Written appraisals should occur at least once a year. Employees should sign the appraisal and have an opportunity to include a written statement. Employees should be given a copy of the evaluation.

4. Provide an employee compensation plan.

In order to maintain fair compensation plans, the municipality should conduct an annual review of salary ranges and benefits at least every three years.

5. Establish an employee suggestion process.

Employees need to be aware of the method established to submit suggestions. These suggestions should be reviewed by elected officials and, where appropriate, department heads.

6. Make professional development available to all staff.

All employees should be eligible for professional development and training within their skill area as well as in the areas of personal development and cultural sensitivity.

7. Verify compliance with all state and federal poster requirements.

Various state and federal agencies require that posters be prominently displayed advising employees of their rights. Your municipality can be cited if you fail to comply. Actions range from a warning to fines that can exceed $1,000.

Required Federal Posters

- Equal Employment Opportunity
- Minimum Wage
- Employee Polygraph Protection Act
- Family & Medical Leave Act
- Job Safety & Health Protection (OSHA or equivalent state poster for public employees).

Required State Posters (varies by state)

- Division of Human Rights
- Minimum Wage
- State Department of Labor/Unemployment Division Registration Number
- Workman's Compensation Certificate of Insurance Coverage for Disability
- Other posters as mandated by each state

8. Formal procedures exist to inform applicants and employees of the notification policy for complaints of discrimination or harassment.

A public procedure is essential to protect applicants, workers and the municipality. In the event of litigation, the first issue raised is whether there is an existing procedure to allow employees to voice their concerns.

Beyond Bare Essentials

Accrediting agencies for various functional areas frequently have sections dedicated to personnel administration. They often are universal and can be used for all departments in a municipality. The Commission on Accreditation for Park and Recreation Agencies and the Commission on Accreditation for Law Enforcement Agencies, Inc., are just two examples. If you have one or more departments that are accredited, you should review and adapt relevant sections.

The following standards were taken from *Self-Assessment Manual for Quality Operation of Park and Recreation Agencies: A Guide to Standards for National Accreditation.*

Written job analysis

- Duties and responsibilities
- Title
- Line of authority
- Scope and range of authority
- Amount and kind of supervision exercised and received
- Tasks required of each position
- Proficiency necessary for each job-related skill special competencies or skills
- Knowledge, abilities, and behaviors
- Education, certification, and experience

Written diversity policy

- Regarding cultural diversity for all employment practices
- Evidence that it is being implemented
- The equal opportunity plan should conduct an annual review of current employment policies, practices, and procedures relevant to their effective impact on the employment and use of all employees

Code of Conduct

- Conflicts of interest
- Partisanship
- Acceptance of gratuities

On-the-Job Training Program

- Evaluated, updated and revised annually

Disciplinary Action

- Unbecoming conduct
- Alcohol and drug use
- Acceptance of gratuities, bribes or rewards
- Abuse of authority
- Proper care and maintenance of equipment

Appeals and Grievances

- Scope of matters that can be grieved
- Time limitations for filing
- Steps in the process
- Criteria for employee representation

Quick Checklist for Human Resources

❑ Develop a personnel policy handbook.

❑ Develop job descriptions for all positions.

❑ Conduct employee performance appraisals.

❑ Provide an employee compensation plan.

❑ Establish an employee suggestion process.

❑ Make professional development available to all staff.

❑ Verify compliance with all state and federal poster requirements.

❑ Formal procedures exist to inform applicants and employees of the notification policy for complaints of discrimination or harassment.

Chapter 6

Park and Recreation Services

Annually, nearly 200 million people use park and recreation services to enhance their physical and social well-being. They seek the highest quality recreation experiences. Public park and recreation departments provide many opportunities for such experiences.

Every public park and recreation department should be concerned with the efficiency, effectiveness, and professionalism of its system. Department self-assessment and peer review is an excellent process for evaluating the quality of the system.

Many municipalities have combined departments of parks and recreation. Typically headed by a director or superintendent of parks and recreation, the two governmental functions can also have their own department head. In this chapter, we treat them as one organization.

Key Sources

Efforts to create standards for the operation of parks and recreation programs and facilities have been under way for more than three decades. In 1965, the National Park and Recreation Association (NRPA) published Standards and Evaluative Criteria for public parks and

---

This chapter is based on materials provided by the National Recreation and Park Association (NRPA).

recreation, which had been developed by a regional practitioner task force. This document was revised in 1972 and reprinted annually for the next 20 years.

In 1989, the National Committee on Accreditation for Park and Recreation Agencies was formed by the Academy for Park and Recreation Administration, with support from Michigan State University, to develop an accreditation program. Faculty at MSU provided facilitating support services. NRPA joined the Academy in the development of the program. Today the NRPA through its Professional Services Division provides administrative services to support the work of the commission.

In 1993, the Commission for Accreditation of Park and Recreation Agencies (CAPRA) was established to be fully responsible for the program, including granting accreditation to departments, training on-site visitors and keeping the standards and commentary up to date. See page eight for an outline of CAPRA's accreditation process.

The commission is an independent body, sanctioned by the Academy and the NRPA. It is composed of 12 members. Four are selected by the Academy, and four by the NRPA. The remaining four seats are filled by representatives from each of the following organizations: the National Association of County Park and Recreation Officials; the International City/County Management Association; the Council of Executive Directors and the American Association for Leisure and Recreation. Members serve a maximum of two three-year terms.

The key source for the standards is the *Self-Assessment Manual For Quality Operation of Park and Recreation Agencies, A Guide to Standards with Commentary and Suggested Evidence of Compliance.*

In addition, the commission has sponsored a resource manual, *Management of Park and Recreation Agencies*, in which the chapters specifically address the content of the standards along with considerable field illustrations. A practitioner and an educator coauthored each chapter.

Other publications include:

- *Department Accreditation and Visitation Procedures for Agencies and Visitation Teams*
- *Agency Accreditation Fact Sheet*, free brochure

Contact Information

National Recreation and Park Association (NRPA)
22377 Belmont Ridge Rd.
Ashburn, VA 20148
703-820-4940
www.activeparks.org

To order publications phone:
703-858-2190
800-626-6772

Bare Essentials

1. Maintain a policy manual.

A manual should list department policies. The manual should be kept up to date. An administrative review should be conducted at least every five years. This manual should be available to pertinent administrative and supervisory personnel.

2. Develop an organizational structure chart.

An organizational structure chart should show interrelationships of staff from highest authority to all staff positions.

3. Develop management information systems.

The department should have management information systems with statistical and data summaries of department activities, such as daily, monthly and annual reports.

4. Keep job descriptions on file.

A written job description for all positions shall be maintained on file. As a minimum these files should include: duties, responsibilities and tasks of each position; minimum level of proficiency necessary in the job-related skills; and knowledge, abilities, and behaviors.

5. Develop on-the-job training.

An on-the-job training program should be developed and then evaluated, updated and revised annually.

6. Establish cash procedures.

There should be procedures for collecting, safeguarding and disbursing cash. These should include: maintenance of an allotment system, if any, or records of appropriations among organization components; preparation of financial statements; conduction of internal audits; and authorization of persons or positions to accept or disperse funds.

7. Establish proper budget procedures.

The department should establish annual operation and capital improvements budgets, including both revenues and expenditures. Procedures for preparation, presentation and adoption of budgets should be standardized.

8. Develop a management plan.

A written maintenance and operations plan for management of the department's park and recreation facilities and equipment should be developed.

9. Develop a general security plan.

A general security plan should be developed for use of outdoor areas, facilities and buildings. Additional plans should exist for specific group program/activity functions.

10. Establish a systematic evaluation program.

A systematic evaluation plan to assess outcomes and the operational efficiency and effectiveness of the department should be developed.

Beyond Bare Essentials

The CAPRA standards, detailed in the *Self-Assessment Manual,* are operational, not quantitative. The standards assess operational park and recreation services practices rather than factors such as availability of funds, land and personnel. The CAPRA standards are comprehensive, covering all aspects of a department's operation rather than specific elements (compared with, for example, population-based open space standards and product-based playground equipment standards). *A thorough self-assessment of an entire department on the basis of the CAPRA standards requires extensive time and effort.*

The 153 standards are divided into 10 categories: Thirty-six of the 153 standards are designated as "fundamental" to quality operations and are required of all departments. Each category includes at least one fundamental standard. Some of the remaining standards may not apply, since specific departments may have only parks and some only recreation. Each department must comply with 85 percent of the non-fundamental standards.

Department Authority, Role and Responsibility
- Source of Authority
- Mission
- Statement of Goals and Objectives
- Relationships

Planning
- Community Planning
- Comprehensive Planning

Organization and Administration
- Organization Structure
- Management Information System
- Public Information, Community Relations

Human Resources

- Chief Administrator
- Personnel Manual
- Professional Considerations

Finance (fiscal policy and management)

- Fiscal Policy

Program and Service Management

- Program/Service Determinants
- Objectives
- Outreach
- Scope of Program Opportunities

Facility and Land Use Management

- Operations and Maintenance
- Natural Resource Management

Safety and Security

- Authority
- Training Program
- General Security Plan

Risk Management

- Risk Management Plan

Evaluation and Research

- Systematic Program
- Training to Conduct Research

Quick Checklist for Park and Recreation Services

❑ Maintain a policy manual.

❑ Develop an organizational structure chart.

❑ Develop management information systems.

❑ Keep job descriptions on file.

❑ Develop on-the-job training.

❑ Establish cash procedures.

❑ Establish proper budget procedures.

❑ Develop a management plan.

❑ Develop a general security plan.

❑ Establish a systematic evaluation program.

Chapter 7

Police Services

Learn About

✓ The changing nature of police services
✓ The Commission on Accreditation for Law Enforcement Agencies, Inc. (CALEA)
✓ Checklist for police services

Police services can be broadly divided into law enforcement and prevention. Enforcement includes the investigation of crimes, recovery of stolen property and the apprehension of suspects. Prevention requires proactive actions based on the analysis of crime trends. Both areas of police services require police departments to maintain higher standards of performance for more services than has been expected in the past.

In the enforcement area, rapid technological changes have led to sophisticated equipment and procedures. Pressures for increased spending and continuous personnel training necessitate the professional analysis of information and the establishment of standards to make difficult choices.

In the prevention area, additional tasks have been added to the functions of local police departments, "Community" and "problem-oriented" policing have become buzz words that are likely to influence police practices permanently. Law enforcement agencies today are expected to participate in diverse crime prevention and education programs. Beginning in first grade with McGruff and Eddie Eagle, on to the fifth grade with the Drug Awareness Resistance Education (D.A.R.E.) program and then into neighborhoods with Crime Watch programs, law enforcement is more integrated into our communities than ever before. Today,

---

This chapter is based on materials provided by the Commission on Accreditation for Law Enforcement Agencies, Inc. (CALEA)

citizens expect a "visible presence" by law enforcement at any major community gathering; not necessarily standing guard over the activities, but as a non-adversarial participant.

In agencies where issues of discipline, accountability and other problems have surfaced, the agencies are at times directed by local government to establish Citizen's Advisory Boards to review policies and practices. In addition, local law enforcement may develop and implement a "Citizen's Academy" or other activities, to allow the community inside the unfamiliar world of law enforcement. The goal is for police departments and their communities to establish open communication and bonds of trust, which will promote greater cooperation.

Key Sources

Several organizations throughout the United States have established law enforcement standards. Some provide accreditation programs at state and local levels. Examples include the Commission for Florida Law Enforcement Accreditation, Inc., New York State Law Enforcement Police Accreditation Program, Massachusetts Police Accreditation Commission, Georgia Police Accreditation Certification, Virginia Law Enforcement Professional Standards Commission.

The most elaborate, well-developed and authoritative standards are available from the Commission on Accreditation for Law Enforcement Agencies, Inc. This organization is generally known by its acronym, CALEA®, and it provides detailed standards that together constitute best practices for law enforcement agencies.

CALEA was formed in 1979 through the combined efforts of four major law enforcement organizations: the International Association of Chiefs of Police, National Organization of Black Law Enforcement Executives, National Sheriff's Association, and Police Executive Research Forum. CALEA is a private, not-for-profit organization working to:

- ◆ Establish professional law enforcement standards
- ◆ Develop and implement a *voluntary* process to achieve compliance with standards
- ◆ Recognize excellence

The first contract was signed in 1983.

CALEA describes 439 standards in their *Standards for Law Enforcement Agencies* manual. Agencies that seek accreditation are required to comply only with those standards that are specifically applicable to them. Applicability is based on two factors: an agency's size and the functions it performs. In order to ensure relevancy, a Standards Review Task Force is established periodically to review standards and make recommendations to the commission for updating the manual.[1]

Because of the growing importance of community relations, CALEA, in conjunction with the Association of Public-Safety Communications Officials-International (APCO®), developed a program with 214 standards specifically designed for public safety communications agencies.[2] The Public-Safety Communications Accreditation, developed in 1998, provides stand-alone and other public safety communications agencies with an opportunity to voluntarily demonstrate their compliance with an established set of professional standards.[3]

The purpose of the Communications Accreditation program is to promote superior public safety communications services and to recognize professional excellence.

CALEA's law enforcement standards and process were the basic profiles used in developing the *Standards for Public Safety Communications Agencies.*[4] PCO provided professional telecommunications leaders and technical experts with appropriately modified standards to meet the specific needs of public safety communications. This is a *separate program* from the one designed to accredit an entire law enforcement agency.

Once an agency signs a contract and pays a fee (required in both programs), the agency conducts a self-assessment to ensure compliance with all applicable standards and gathers proofs of compliance for later verification by the on-site assessment team. The agency is assisted in this process with instruction and guidance from the Commission staff. The assessment teams are trained and selected by CALEA.

This independent audit occurs every three years throughout the duration of the agency's accredited status. Maintaining compliance with the CALEA standards is the final component of both accreditation programs.

---

[1] *Standards for Law Enforcement Agencies: The Standards Manual of the Law Enforcement Agency Accreditation Program,* 4th ed. (CALEA, January 1, 1999)

[2] *Accreditation Program Overview.* (Commission on Accreditation for Law Enforcement Agencies, Inc., 1999)

[3] *Standards for Public Safety Communications Agencies,* (CALEA, January, 1999)

[4] Ibid.

┌─────────────────────────────────┐
│ **Contact Information** │
│   │
│ **The Commission on Accreditation** │
│ **for Law Enforcement Agencies, Inc. (CALEA)** │
│   │
│ Sylvester Daughtry, Jr.   10306 Eaton Place │
│ *Executive Director*   Fairfax, VA 22030 │
│   │
│ Peg Gant   www.calea.org │
│ *Program Manager*   800-368-3757 │
│ pgant@calea.org   703-352-4225 │
└─────────────────────────────────┘

Bare Essentials

1. Complete state or national accreditation process.

State government or not-for-profit agencies (such as CALEA) will certify that the department has met established standards for that organization.

2. Conduct customer surveys at least once a year.

Customer satisfaction surveys should be conducted on an annual or biannual basis to determine the quality of service and the department's responsiveness to the community.

Citizens' surveys are a tool many outstanding agencies use to determine if the communities they serve like, *and support*, their agencies. A policy requiring the agency to periodically survey the community served and implement a procedure for gathering and analyzing that data will help an agency remain responsive to the community's needs and concerns. A survey of community members having direct contact with the department is preferred, although general population surveys are also useful.

3. Maintain a high case clearance rate.

Clearance rate refers to the number of investigated criminal cases that are resolved. A case can be cleared by arrest, identification of a suspect with no arrest, a change of status from crime to accident, and any other process an agency uses to close out a case. A department's clearance rate should be equal to or higher than the mean of the clearance rates for departments in the same region.

4. Obtain feedback from employees and the public.

The department should have a suggestion system for use by employees and the public. Establish a process to inform the staff and the public of the suggestions submitted and the actions that result.

5. Maintain a clearly defined and adequately funded community involvement program.

Involvement between law enforcement and the community is much more complex and demanding. A professional law enforcement agency will initiate programs that provide a forum for constructive dialog with citizens. This would include embracing the community oriented policing or problem oriented policing philosophies, as well as some form of citizen's academy or other activities. The primary purpose of a citizen's academy is to encourage citizens to get to know their law enforcement agency and how it functions. This is an excellent way to build bridges of trust and acceptance between the community and the police.

Although a citizen's academy is not necessarily required to meet this standard, the goal of the academy is. For that reason, it is useful to provide some detail on the idea. Developed during the 1990s, the Academy is set up to allow the citizen-participant to attend during the evening, on a set schedule of one or two nights per week for two to four hours per session. This will allow for participants who are employed during the day or children and/or spouses to attend, as well as retired citizens. The academy is usually operated at a relatively small cost, calling upon agency personnel for instruction, utilizing agency facilities and equipment, and providing all materials needed to the participants at no or low cost.

6. Establish clear procedures for handling complaints.

A law enforcement agency should notify the community of the procedure for registering complaints *and* compliments. The agency should also have a policy and procedure for investigating complaints against agency members, notifying the member of the complaint, concluding the investigation and notifying the complainant and the agency member of the results and action to be taken, if any.

7. Promote nondiscriminatory personnel policies.

In today's litigious society, lawsuits regarding discrimination in hiring and promotional practices are increasingly likely. A law enforcement agency that reports few legal actions against them in this area has most certainly developed equitable policies and procedures on recruiting, hiring, training and promotional opportunities for all agency personnel. This may be viewed as a minimum standard of performance. Law enforcement agencies are encouraged to develop proactive programs that protect job candidates and current employees from discriminatory practices.

Beyond Bare Essentials

The following are the major topic headings in the *Standards For Law Enforcement Agencies* manual, Fourth Edition. In addition, selected chapters of functions covered by these standards are listed under the appropriate topic. There are 439 standards in the Fourth edition manual. This sample is meant to illustrate the broad range of functions within a law enforcement agency that should be considered.

Law Enforcement Roles, Responsibilities and Relationships

- Law Enforcement Agency Role
- Limits of Authority
- Use of Force
- Agency Jurisdiction and Mutual Aid
- Contractual Agreements

Organization, Management and Administration

- Organizational Structure
- Authority and Responsibility
- Goals and Objectives
- Planning and Research
- Written Directives
- Crime Analysis
- Allocation and Distribution of Personnel

The Personnel Structure

- Collective Bargaining and Contract Management
- Grievance Procedures
- Disciplinary Procedures

The Personnel Process

- Equal Employment Opportunity and Recruitment
- Recruit Training

- Specialized In-service Training
- Professional and Legal Requirements (Promotion)

Law Enforcement Operations

- Patrol
- Criminal Investigation
- Vice, Drugs and Organized Crime
- Juvenile Operations
- Crime Prevention and Community Involvement
- Unusual Occurrences and Special Operations

Operations Support

- Internal Affairs
- Public Information

Traffic Operations

Prisoner and Court-Related Activities

Auxiliary and Technical Services

- Communications
- Records
- Collection and Preservation of Evidence
- Property and Evidence Control

Quick Checklist for Police Services

❏ **Complete state or national accreditation process.**

❏ **Conduct customer surveys at least once a year.**

❏ **Maintain a high case clearance rate.**

❏ **Obtain feedback from employees and the public.**

❏ **Maintain a clearly defined and adequately funded community involvement program.**

❏ **Establish clear procedures for handling complaints.**

❏ **Promote nondiscriminatory personnel policies.**

Chapter 8

Property Assessment

The property assessor plays a critical role in ensuring a local government's fiscal health. Assessments based on current market values can strengthen fiscal health by:

◆ *Maximizing potential property tax revenues.* Inadequate assessment practices generally underestimate property values, thereby limiting potential property tax revenues by understating the tax base.

◆ *Increasing borrowing capacity.* General underassessment restricts the power to use bond financing, which is often limited to a specific ratio of debt to total assessed value. Assessed value also influences bond rating; higher assessed values can result in higher bond ratings and a lower interest rate.

◆ *Assuring a full share of intergovernmental aid.* Intergovernmental payments to local government are often tied to property values. Aid distribution formulas penalize local governments that understate property values.

Assessment offices are a key, and often the only point of contact between citizens and government. The work of the assessor can generate attitudes that may spill over into a general attitude toward government. Fair, open, efficient administration of assessments is the most important element in making the taxpayer's experience satisfactory. A courteous staff trained to deal with the public, written rules of procedure and an office layout accessible to the public are essential.

This chapter is based on material provided by the International Association of Assessing Officers.

Distinguishing between property assessment and taxation is important, both for local officials evaluating the performance of the office and for the taxpayer trying to understand or appeal an assessment. Property assessors locate and describe properties or appraise the value of all properties, keep records linking properties to prospective owners and designate the official value for tax purposes, taking into account legal reasons for changing appraised values. Other government officials are responsible for setting property tax rates and levies. These officials determine the total amount to be raised by the property tax, while the property assessor determines the distribution of the property tax burden among taxpayers according to the value of property.

Key Sources

The most authoritative source for deriving benchmarks for your assessment office is the International Association of Assessing Officers (IAAO). A not-for-profit educational institution, the mission of the IAAO is to promote innovation and excellence in property appraisal, property tax policy and administration through professional development, education, research and technical assistance. The IAAO sets standards, conducts research, provides education and technical assistance and certifies individuals through its designation program.

Contact Information

International Association of Assessing Officers (IAAO)
130 E. Randolph, Suite 850
Chicago, IL 60601
www.iaao.org
312-819-6100

The type of information you will need varies by state. Oversight agencies in most states often provide information on standards of performance and on the performance of assessment offices. State associations or agencies often certify or accredit assessors according to statutory requirements.

Bare Essentials

1. Maintain appropriate appraisal levels and require uniformity in all assessing.

Because the role of the assessment office is to distribute the tax burden fairly, according to the value of property, measures of appraisal level and uniformity can indicate the quality of performance. We recommend the following two performance measures.

Appraisal level refers to the ratio of appraised value to an independent estimate of market value, such as sale price. For example, if the assessor appraises a property at $90,000 and the market value is $100,000, the ratio is $90,000/$100,000, or 0.9. In mass appraisals, appraised values cannot be expected to equal 1.0, but low and high ratios should balance so that the typical ratio should be close to 1.0. *The overall level of appraisal for the jurisdiction should be within 10 percent of the level required by law.* If properties are reappraised infrequently, the level of appraisal is likely to be poor.

Appraisal uniformity relates to the fair and equitable treatment of individual properties. *Uniformity requires equitable treatment both within and between groups of properties.* Uniformity among groups can be measured by comparing appraisal levels. Sometimes, statutes provide that different classes of property are to be assessed at different percentages of market value. But, if all classes of property are required to be appraised at 100 percent of market value and residential property is appraised at 90 percent, while vacant land is appraised at 60 percent, the result is that vacant land is under-appraised relative to residential property. When this occurs, owners of vacant land will pay about one-third less per dollar of market value, less than their fair share of taxes.

Uniformity within groups is determined by measuring the size of the differences between each ratio and the average or middle ratio. The importance of uniformity within groups can be seen by looking at the example below.

Examples of Appraisal Uniformity

In Group 1, the largest difference between ratios is 0.20 (1.10 – 0.90), but in Group 2 it is 1.20 (1.60 – 0.40). Although the average ratio is the same in both groups, uniformity is better in Group 1 than in Group 2; therefore, tax burdens will be more uniformly distributed among property owners.

	Group 1	Group 2
	0.90	0.40
	0.95	0.80
	1.00	1.00
	1.05	1.20
	1.10	1.60
Average	1.00	1.00

Appraisal uniformity is measured by statistics such as the coefficient of dispersion (COD). Here is a list of ideal CODs for six types of properties:

- Single-family homes and condominiums should be 15 or less.
- New or fairly similar residences should be 10 or less.
- Income-producing properties should be 20 or less.

- ◆ Larger, urban jurisdictions should be 15 or less.
- ◆ Vacant land should be 20 or less.
- ◆ Heterogeneous rural residential property and seasonal homes should be 20 or less.

2. Encourage certification of assessing officers.

At least one employee of the assessment office should be certified by the state or hold a professional designation. Ideally, every officer would be certified.

3. Conduct customer surveys to ensure satisfaction.

Citizen satisfaction with the assessor's office should be high. Level of satisfaction is systematically measured by frequent customer surveys available to citizens at the point of service or by follow-up mail. Confidentiality should be protected. A sample customer survey can be viewed on the previous page. Feel free to duplicate this survey for use in any of your government offices.

Assessment Office Comment Card

Date Visited: / / /   Time Visited:

Location Visited: Who Assisted You?

The Overall Service Was: ❏ Excellent   ❏ Good   ❏ Fair   ❏ Poor

Comments:

How might we better serve you in the future?

May we contact you in the future about your response so that we can improve our service?   ❏ Yes   ❏ No

If you marked "yes", please provide your name and telephone number:

Name:

Daytime Phone: Evening Phone:

Thank you for your time.

Beyond Bare Essentials

If the checklist points out problems with the assessment office or if you have concerns with its operations for other reasons, you should enlist the cooperation of other elected officials and the assessor for a more detailed study. The IAAO's *Assessment Practices Self-Evaluation Guide* provides a checklist for examining every aspect of the assessment office. You can prioritize the list according to what you and your colleagues determine to be appropriate and important. Examples of some of these standards are below. A complete list can be obtained from IAAO, which continuously revises its publications.

Mapping and Land Information

- Are maps drawn using professionally accepted standards for size, scale, layout, lines, symbols and the like?
- Do you maintain data on land attributes (for example, neighborhood, land use topography, soil type and view)?

Commercial Property Valuation

- Except for unique, special-purpose properties, do you use at least two valuation approaches for each property?
- In the cost approach, have base rates and cost factors been developed from local cost data or adjusted to the local market?

Personal Property Assessment

- Are your personal property reporting forms tailored to the needs of different businesses and industries?
- Do you use price guides to value items that are often sold used?

Tax Administration

- Do you update ownership and legal description information in your records within 30 days of a sale being recorded?
- Do you verify eligibility for exemptions?

Public Information and Relations

- Can property records be accessed by parcel identifier, address and owner?
- Do you have available to the public a nontechnical description of how property is assessed, appeal rights and procedures, exemptions and other forms of tax relief as well as how property tax bills are calculated?

Assessment Appeal

- Do you notify property owners by mail of the amount and reason for changes in assessed values, as well as of their rights to appeal?
- Do you track the status of each formal appeal to ensure that it is appropriately disposed of and that records are properly updated?

Quick Checklist for Property Assessment

❏ Maintain appropriate appraisal levels and require uniformity in all assessing.

❏ Encourage certification of assessing officers.

❏ Conduct customer surveys to ensure satisfaction.

Chapter 9

Public Works Agencies

Learn About

✓ **The variety of services provided by public works agencies**

✓ **The American Public Works Association (APWA) and the information available on recommended practices**

✓ **Checklist for public works agencies**

Public works is the broadly defined area dedicated to the management of publicly owned infrastructure. This infrastructure literally ranges from A to Z – airports to zoos. The general public usually thinks of public works as streets and highways, bridges, sewers, water systems, parks and solid waste.

Public works departments are frequently charged with the management of airports, buildings (including schools and hospitals), cemeteries, code enforcement (including building and zoning permits), development and subdivisions, drainage and flood control, electrical generation and distribution, equipment (including police and fire vehicles), hazardous waste response, natural gas, parking enforcement, planning, traffic control, and yes – even zoos. Understanding of the public works field is often complicated by the fact that many public agencies don't have a central public works department, but rather several departments, each with a separate name – none of which may be called "public works."

Because of the broad range of functions, the guidelines we provide are broad and aimed at general processes rather than specific performance measures. Our goal is to help you conduct initial explorations to find out if your public works department needs further study. As you will see by reviewing the topics covered in the last section of this chapter,

This chapter is based on material provided by the American Public Works Association (APWA).

a comprehensive study would require considerable resources. It probably would make more sense to review specific operations such as trash removal or highways before undertaking a comprehensive analysis.

Key Sources

The American Public Works Association (APWA) represents federal, state, provincial, regional and local government public works agencies and their private sector counterparts throughout the U.S. and Canada. The association provides education, networking, advocacy and public information for both members and the general public. In 1996, the APWA approved the establishment of an accreditation program designed to recognize public works agencies that complied with recommended practices developed by an international consortium of public works professionals.

Accreditation is a voluntary process offered through the Accreditation Council, the accreditation-granting arm of the APWA. The council is comprised of professional managers with public and private sector experience in the delivery of government services. Since self-assessment and accreditation are voluntary, each public works agency has the ability to select how far they wish to proceed in the process. An agency can choose to participate only in the self-assessment process as a needs assessment or quality improvement program.

To become accredited, agencies must comply with all of the recommended practices of the APWA. The recommended practices are contained in the *Public Works Management Practices Manual*. In its third edition, the manual contains over 460 recommended practices, separated into 31 chapters – each dealing with one area that public works departments might be responsible for managing. Agencies only need to comply with the practices that they are responsible for managing.

Any government agency responsible for managing public works infrastructure and services is eligible for accreditation. Major departments or divisions within large agencies can be accredited individually. There are no limits on the number of departments or divisions that can apply for accreditation.

The American Public Works Association is an international educational and professional association of public agencies, private sector companies and individuals dedicated to providing high quality public works goods and services.

Originally chartered in 1937, the APWA is the largest and oldest organization of its kind in the world, with headquarters in Kansas City, MO, an office in Washington, D.C., and 67 chapters throughout North America. The APWA provides a forum in which public works professionals can exchange ideas, improve professional competency, increase the performance of their agencies and companies, and bring important public works-related topics to public attention in local, state and federal arenas.

The association is a highly participatory organization, with hundreds of opportunities for leadership and service and a network of several dozen national committees in every area of public works. Governed by a 17-member board of directors, elected at both the regional and national levels, the APWA is an open, flexible association with a diverse membership of 26,000 and a reputation for quality services and products.

Contact Information

The American Public Works Association
2345 Grand Boulevard, Suite 500
Kansas City, MO 64108-2641

Website: www.apwa.net
Email: apwa@apwa.net

816-472-6100
Fax: 472-1610

Bare Essentials

This section lists written documents or specific policies that any professional public works agency should have in place. They will help scratch the surface to see if your government needs additional study and evaluation. They are stated in specific terms, but the *Public Works Management Practices Manual*[1] will provide a more complete description.

1. Maintain up-to-date mission and vision statements.

The agency's mission statement is a concise description of the fundamental purpose for which the agency exists. This statement answers the questions of why the agency exists and whom the agency is serving. Mission statements for the fundamental areas (streets, water supply, solid waste management, etc.) may also be developed.

The agency's vision statement describes the vision of the agency's leadership. The role of a leader is to create a vision and set a course for moving toward that dream. Leaders convert dreams into reality. This statement answers questions about what the leadership of the agency wants to create and the direction of the agency.

---

[1] Recommended Statements are from the *Public Works Management Practices Manual, 3rd Edition*, 1998, the American Public Works Association (ISBN 0-917084-71-3).

The agency's value statement establishes the core values, which will assist in fulfilling the mission of the agency. This statement answers questions about the culture the leadership of the agency wants to create and how all agency employees are to act. The values are tangible behaviors, which define how each employee is expected to act.

2. Set and meet training goals for each job classification.

Training goals should be consistent with the agency's mission, vision and value statements. These goals provide the basis for developing all training programs, choosing teaching methods and evaluating performance. A written plan should detail how these goals will be met.

3. Make capital planning and improvement program available to public.

The capital planning program should identify how the capital plan fits into the established policies, goals and objectives; and how the capital improvement process incorporates engineering and finance recommendations. A financial analysis may be performed to determine the potential to carry out a capital plan, identify financing methods and funding sources, and assess funding availability and constraints. Input from all governing boards should be included in a capital improvement program.

4. Make available and follow a public written plan for multi-hazard emergency response.

Effective emergency response and recovery can only be achieved through a comprehensive multi-hazard plan. The plan must involve all government service providers and community groups that contribute to meeting emergency needs. Emergency plans should include statements regarding mission, intent of plan, description of the organization, emergency resources, and provisions for outside assistance. The plan should detail emergency policies, procedures, responsibilities and communications.

5. Identify personnel responsible for inspecting equipment and vehicles.

Job descriptions should outline the inspection functions and levels of expertise of personnel so that the scope of responsibilities for inspections is clear.

6. Use a schedule to designate the time and frequency of trash collections.

Customers are notified of collection schedules for all classes of materials collected, as well as routine schedule changes because of holidays or other events. Specify times for setting out filled containers and retrieving emptied containers to enhance public health and neighborhood appearances. Make sure a viable enforcement mechanism is in place.

7. Clearly and publicly state operations and maintenance procedures and standards.

Establish procedures for conducting operations and maintenance activities. These are based on accepted industry practices, local resources (maintenance funds, labor and equipment), environmental issues and other local conditions that may affect practices such as terrain, street network and climate. Performance standards indicate how operations and maintenance activities will be accomplished with available resources. These standards may be integrated within a maintenance management system that ties available resources to workload. Performance standards define a realistic rate of accomplishment, which results from applying resources with the use of the best procedures for work activities. Accepted operation and maintenance standards are identified and used for street functions such as pothole repair, traffic control devices, street lighting, bridges, retaining walls and pedestrian facilities.

Beyond Bare Essentials

The abridged table of contents below[1] provides some of the guidelines for areas of government operations under the general category of public works. You can obtain the complete publication from the APWA.

Organization
- Mission, Vision, Value Statements
- Organizational Policies
- Code of Ethics

Personnel Management
- Career Development Practices and Procedures
- Training Evaluation
- Affirmative Action Plan

Planning
- Strategic Planning Process
- Planning Goals and Objectives
- Plan Monitoring

Finance
- Cost of Service
- Forecasting Capital Improvements
- Contracts

Risk Management and Legal Review
- Claims
- Legal Review
- Ordinance and Regulations Enforcement

Communications
- Communication with Governing Boards
- Communication with Public

Records
- Records Management
- Access to Records
- Data Security

Safety
- Safety Measures and Reports
- Safety Awards
- Safety Training

---

[1] Recommended Statements are from the *Public Works Management Practices Manual, 3rd Edition*, 1998, the American Public Works Association (ISBN 0-917084-71-3).

Municipal Engineering
* Land Use Planning
* Plan Review
* Construction Management

Engineering Design
* Design Standards
* Quality Assurance Plan and Design Review
* Contract Documents

Bid Process
* Contractor Qualification
* Bid Evaluation
* Bid Award/Rejection

Construction
* Construction Management
* Inspection
* Measurement and Payment

Right-of-Way Permits
* Permit Issuance
* Permit Process
* Permit Inspection

Utility Coordination
* Utility Coordination
* Long-range Utility Planning
* Utility Maps and Records

Buildings
* Maintenance Program
* Preventive Maintenance
* Maintenance Quality

Equipment Operator Qualifications
* Parts Inventory
* Equipment Specifications
* Specification/Bid Analysis

Grounds
* Landscape Management
* Cemeteries (Practice superseded by "Cemeteries" section)
* Playgrounds

Parking Lots
* Parking Lot Planning
* Parking Lot Design
* Parking Lot Maintenance

Solid Waste Management
* Solid Waste Plan
* Source Reduction
* Environmental Compliance

Solid Waste Collection
* Quality of Service
* Collection Days and Set-Out Time
* Routing

Solid Waste Processing
* Recycling
* Composting Program
* Resource Recovery Operations

Solid Waste Disposal
* Landfill Design
* Environmental Monitoring
* Odor

Streets
* Operations and Maintenance Procedures and Standards
* Infrastructure Condition
* Preventive Maintenance

Street Cleaning
* Quality of Service
* Routing
* Litter Control

Snow Removal and Ice Control
* Snow and Ice Control Plan
* Equipment Preparation
* Spreading and Plowing Procedures

Stormwater and Flood Management
* Stormwater and Flood Management Service Levels
* Operation Plan
* Public Education

Potable Water
* Water Quality or Quantity Changes
* Infrastructure Location
* Incentives for Water Conservation

Wastewater
* Wastewater Treatment Requirements
* Operations Manual
* Long-Range System Planning

Traffic Operation Traffic Policy and Procedures Manual
* Petition for Installation of Traffic Control Devices
* Sign Installation Policy
* Special Signs

Cemeteries
* Interment, Inurnment and Scattering
* Mapping Blocks
* Marketing and Pre-Need Sales

Quick Checklist for Public Works Agencies

❏ Maintain up-to-date mission and vision statements.

❏ Set and meet training goals for each job classification.

❏ Make capital planning and improvement program available to public.

❏ Make available and follow a public written plan for multi-hazard emergency response.

❏ Identify personnel responsible for inspecting equipment and vehicles.

❏ Use a schedule to designate the time and frequency of trash collections.

❏ Clearly and publicly state operations and maintenance procedures and standards.

Chapter 10

Web Site Design

Learn About

✓ **Basic functions of developing a Web site**

✓ **Help to get started**

✓ **Seven bare essentials**
   Checklist for Web site design

✓ **Model Web sites**

Growing numbers of citizens rely on the Internet as their news source. Email has replaced the phone for many people, who also rely on the World Wide Web for shopping, banking and conducting research. It is natural that government move in this direction. The resources dedicated to Web site maintenance can be justified by the staff time that might otherwise be spent making copies, looking up information or responding to requests for forms. Citizens seeking information will no longer be confined to the inconvenience of normal business hours. Inquiries can also be answered via email.

There are few limits to the type of information that can appear on a Web site:

- ◆ Assessment rolls and related information
- ◆ Property tax information
- ◆ Meeting notices, agendas and minutes
- ◆ Municipal budget
- ◆ Zoning ordinances
- ◆ Forms
- ◆ Fees
- ◆ Listing of all elected officials and department heads, email addresses and phone numbers

If it's a public record, it probably belongs on your Web site. In some municipalities citizens can pay their property taxes, water bills or permit fees via the Internet using credit or debit cards.

Regardless of how well you know your constituents, they may see their level of access to government as limited. What opportunities do people have to look at the budget or the minutes of a recent meeting? What if they are interested in viewing the municipal zoning codes or in applying for a building permit? What about a businessperson scouting out new locations, potential tourists or homebuyers? A well-designed Web site may make the difference for each of these audiences.

Regardless of the value of having a Web site, you may still feel that the financial and labor costs are too high. If this is the case, you may want to identify a corporate sponsor or a web design/maintenance company that will cover the expense in exchange for advertising space on your Web site. If you live in a community with a college or university, explore the opportunities that might be available to have a student or team of students design and maintain (at least initially) your Web site as an internship for college credit. You should also ask that the student(s) train your staff and produce an easy to follow guide that will allow the staff to update the Web site on a regular basis. Another option is to ask the information studies faculty/staff to recommend the names of students that you can hire. Finally, you may want to consider sending staff members to a Web design course. Web software is often as easy to use as word processing programs.

Key Sources

Web site development is increasing exponentially, and so are the resources to support this growth. The following is not an exhaustive list, but are sources you may want to consider. All are Web sites except for the last reference.

http://www.maxwell.syr.edu/benchmarks/

Municipal Web Sites in Onondaga County: A Study Comparing Selected Characteristics evaluates local municipal sites and provides a how-to guide for creating a Web site. One of several publications based on local research projects conducted by the Community Benchmarks Program at Syracuse University's Maxwell School of Citizenship and Public Affairs.

http://www.hotwired.com/webmonkey/

Webmonkey is a resource for Web developers, but it can be used by anyone. While emerging technologies and trends are one focus, the site also includes tutorials that walk you through the basics. You can check out how-to projects, articles and commentaries or subscribe to *Elbow Grease*, the Web site's newsletter.

http://www.builder.com/Business/Rules/

'Netiquette,' a helpful guide to Web etiquette.

http://www.cnet.com

Tips and a how-to library are available for Web building and Web services, along with rankings of the top Internet Service Providers.

http://www.websitetips.com/designer/index.html

The a-z of creating your own Web site, including legal issues.

http://www.aaecommercesolutions.com/bullet_tips.htm

Learn about keyword searches, metatags and search engine submissions.

http://directory.google.com/Top/Computers/Graphics?Web_Graphics/ Free_Graphics/

An interactive site that allows you to download free backgrounds and buttons along with tips, ideas and advice.

http://www.cast.org/bobby/

Evaluation of the accessibility of your site to people with disabilities.

Castro, Elizabeth. *HTML for the World Wide Web*. Peachpit Press. 1998.

A guide to HTML, Photoshop, images, forms, lists, tables, links, frames, multimedia and color. The book provides excellent examples and is easy to follow.

Bare Essentials

The goal is to develop and maintain a Web site that is user friendly. The standards listed represent the basic components of a quality Web site.

1. **The municipality has a Web site.**

2. **The Web site is updated monthly.**

3. **Notices, agendas and minutes of all meetings are posted.**

4. **A list of all departments and, where appropriate, a description of services is provided.**

5. **Names, phone numbers and email addresses are provided for all department heads and elected officials.**

6. **The Web site provides users with an opportunity to submit comments, questions, or suggestions, as well as direct email capability to department heads and elected officials.**

7. **Every link functions properly.**

Beyond Bare Essentials

Bare Essentials provides you with the information standards for a Web site while this section gives you the characteristics of an effective and efficient site.

The Web site describes the steps necessary to obtain permits and licenses as well as fees charged.

The Web site provides a functioning keyword search engine.

- Users are able to search the Web site by inputting key words.

The Web site has persistent navigation.

- Users can consistently locate navigation links to pages on the Web site, normally buttons on the upper left side of each page.

Users are able to easily return to the homepage from each linking page.

- Through an icon on each page, not the browser's back button.

Web site is designed so that it will adjust to the screen size and format of different browsers.

- Tested by using a minimum of three popular web browsers to search for the municipal Web site.

The municipal Web site is registered with several popular search engines.

- This gives users searching for the Web site the ability to locate the municipality using a key word search.

Model Web Sites

The Web sites on the following page were the winners of Government Technology's fourth annual Best of Web contest. The entries were evaluated by representatives from Government Technology, the National Association of Counties, the North Dakota League of Cities, the International City/County Management Association, Public Technology Inc. and State Technologies. The winners were chosen based on user-friendliness, the amount of information available, and convenience. Judges selected six winning web sites and several honorable mentions, out of over 120 entries. Top sites are quick-loading, easy-to-navigate, and often include features such as online transactions and downloadable forms and applications.

Best of the Web Winners 1998[1]

- Pennsylvania
  www.state.pa.us
- Connecticut
  www.state.ct.us
- Georgia
  www.state.ga.us
- Missouri Department of Economic
  Development
  www.ecodev.state.mo.us
- Florida Department of Transportation
  www.dot.state.fl.us
- City of Indianapolis/Marion County
  www.IndyGov.org
- Seattle
  www.ci.seattle.wa.us
- Chicago
  www.ci.chicago.il.us
- Howard County
  www.co.ho.md.us
- City and County of San Francisco
  www.ci.sf.ca.us

Best of the Web Winners 1999[2]

- State of Washington
  http://access.wa.gov
- State of Georgia
  **www.gagovernor.org/governor/
  firstlady/**
- State of South Dakota
  www.state.sd.us

- State of Maryland
  www.dllr.state.md.us/license
- State of Delaware
  www.state.de.us
- City of Boston
  www.ci.boston.ma.us
- City of Chicago
  www.cityofchicago.org
- San Diego County
  www.co.san-diego.ca.us
- City and County of San Francisco
  www.ci.sf.ca.us
- City of Gaithersburg, Marlyland
  www.ci.gaithersburg

General Websites

- Erie County
  www.erie.gov
- Internet Dot Com
  www.internet.com
- Monroe County
  www.co.monroe.ny.us
- New York State Office for
  Technology
  www.irm.state.ny.us/trend
- New York State Office of Regulatory
  Reform
  www.gorr.state.ny.us/gorr
- Onondaga County Website
  www.co.onondaga.ny.us

---

[1] Source: *Government Technology: Government Internet Guide.* October 1998 and October 1999.

[2] Ibid.

Quick Checklist for Web Site Design

❏ The municipality has a Web site.

❏ The Web site is updated monthly.

❏ Notices, agendas and minutes of all meetings are posted.

❏ A list of departments and, where appropriate, a description of services is provided.

❏ Names, phone numbers and email addresses are provided for all department heads and elected officials.

❏ The Web site provides users with an opportunity to submit comments, questions, or suggestions, as well as direct email capability to department heads and elected officials.

❏ Every link functions properly.

Benchmarking
Made Easy

Unless you are keeping score, it is difficult to know whether you are winning or losing. This applies to ball games, card games, and no less to government . . .

Harry Hatry, *The Urban Institute*

Using the checklists for effective government is only the first step. In Part Two, we provide you with additional tools to take the next step on the road to continuous improvement. These chapters will help you measure both resources and results.

Chapter 11

Why Should Elected Officials Benchmark?

The short answer for the question in the chapter title is that benchmarking will improve government because it organizes information to facilitate continuous improvement. As you will see, we use "benchmarks" as a level of performance we seek to meet. It is the same idea as a golfer seeking to have a lower score the next time out, an investor seeking to raise the return on investment or a car buyer shopping for the lowest price. A benchmark is a target to shoot for in getting government costs under control or improving the quality of government services. If you don't have a target and are not careful about measuring your progress, you are not serious about continuous improvement.

Purists will question our use of the term "benchmarking." They see benchmarking as a rigorous business practice where a best practice is identified and the performance associated with the best practice is clearly measured. Some type of comparison is implicit in the purist version so that the level sought is at least in the top 10 percent. This formal and pure use of the term is not universal, especially in the world of government. In fact, the popular media increasingly uses the term in the general way described in this book. As we will discuss, a benchmark can be chosen because it makes sense to those in charge.

Benchmarking Defined

Benchmarks, as defined in this guide, consist of two parts:

- **Indicators** that measure some condition.
- **A goal** for that condition. Benchmarks are best thought of as measurable objectives, a structured method of evaluation.

Benchmarking is equivalent to using a thermometer to see if you have a fever. Your temperature tells you if you are sick. If your temperature is above normal, you would take remedial action – two aspirins.

Benchmarking is evaluation with a purpose: to help government officials improve their performance. We can adapt what the authors said in *Reinventing Government*[1] to describe the benefits of evaluation:

- What gets benchmarked gets done.
- If you don't benchmark results, you can't tell success from failure.
- If you can't see success, you can't learn from it.
- If you can demonstrate results, you can win support.

Getting a clear fix on the current situation and a future goal in measurable terms can create a target on which all can agree. As an elected official, you can use benchmarking to help increase your effectiveness as a leader.

Frequently Asked Questions (FAQs)

FAQ #1: Do We Really Need to Use Such a Technical Name?

Why use such an unusual word like "benchmarking?" Why not call it "setting goals" or "measuring costs and performance"? We prefer the term for the following reasons, all of which have to do with communicating and gaining support.

- *Benchmarking* is shorter and easier to say than "setting goals that can be clearly measured."
- *Benchmarking* sounds official and formal, but is easy to pronounce and carries intuitive meaning.
- *Benchmarking* always forces the question "What's the benchmark?" People may not like to be pinned down by stating clear goals. The question keeps everyone focused.

---

[1] Osborne, David and Ted Gaebler. *Reinventing Government: How the Entrepreneurial Spirit is Transforming the Public Sector.* New York: Plume, 1993, 146-155.

- *Benchmarking* serves the same purpose as keeping score in baseball. It becomes a rallying point for team members to work together.

These four reasons capture the powerful logic of continuous improvement encompassed in the idea of benchmarking. Continuous improvement can be achieved only if the work and results of the organization are monitored through careful measurement and if goals are set. "Measurable goals" is just another way of saying "benchmarks." Benchmarking has worked wonders in business and is starting to do the same in government and the not-for-profit world.

FAQ #2: What Can Benchmarks Measure?

The short answer is *anything*: that goes for your own personal life (like your temperature); your neighborhood; local municipality; state; the country and even the world. We have created five general categories of benchmarks used in assessing local government:

 1. The Cost of Government Services

 2. The Workload of Government Services

 3. The Efficiency of Government Services

 4. The Quality of Government Services

 5. The Quality of Life in Your Community

FAQ #3: What's an Indicator and What's a Benchmark?

Indicators are clear descriptions of what governments do and how well they do it. They can be qualitative, such as whether or not the clerk's office conducts customer surveys, or quantitative, such as the per capita cost of police services in a given year.

Indicators become benchmarks when goals are set. If you and your colleagues want the clerk to conduct customer surveys, the benchmark would be "customer surveys are conducted." If you and your colleagues want per capita cost of police services to be no more than the county average, then that average becomes the benchmark.

Benchmarking resembles the idea of a thermometer. Think of replacing degrees of heat, a measurement, with something related to government, such as the cost of trash collection, response time to a fire alarm, or satisfaction with the service in a clerk's office. Then determine the level of performance that the agency should meet. In other words, set your benchmark.

Body Heat: Temperature

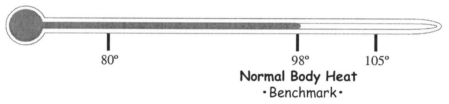

80°   98°   105°

Normal Body Heat
• Benchmark •

Trash Collection: Cost Per Household

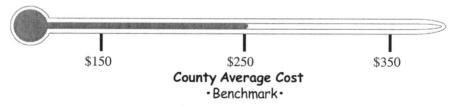

$150 $250 $350

County Average Cost
• Benchmark •

Fire Department: Response Time

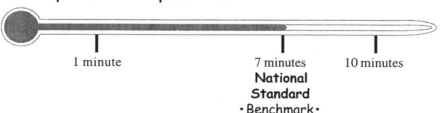

1 minute   7 minutes   10 minutes

**National
Standard**
• Benchmark •

FAQ #4: Isn't Choosing Benchmarks Political?

The answer is an emphatic "yes." Choosing benchmarks is a way to communicate with your constituents in order to determine what is important to them and what should be accomplished to improve society. That is the purpose of politics in a democracy. Citizens, other elected officials, government managers and workers can openly exchange views about how they feel society should improve because benchmarking requires a clear statement of goals and how they will be measured. This exchange can be grounded in specifics rather than floating around in abstract ideological debate. As a someone trying to improve government, you should welcome the clarity benchmarking brings to your efforts.

Benchmarking Examples

The point of these two examples is to show that benchmarking creates a less emotional and more concrete way for citizens and government officials to evaluate government services so that the actual performance becomes the basis for discussion.

Trash Collection

 Our benchmarking study on the cost of trash collection for 35 municipalities in upstate New York revealed that the average cost was highest for residents who had to contract with a commercial hauler for individual service. Average cost was lowest for residents who lived in municipalities that contracted with a hauler on behalf of all citizens. The study's findings stimulated public awareness of the trade-offs of each type of service and helped citizens understand how government could help. As a result, several towns are now moving toward more efficient and less costly municipally-contracted services.

Political Campaign

We developed a countywide report of government services in six departments, ranking the results. During the next election, an incumbent town supervisor, whose town received high marks, used our findings as part of her campaign for re-election. The report provided the basis for a political strategy that might encourage public trust.

FAQ #5: If I don't feel comfortable using the term "benchmarking," can I still use the basic idea behind it?

If benchmarking becomes a household word among government officials and citizens, we would be both ecstatic and astonished. Our local governments would be more efficient and cost effective. This would mean that the philosophy of continuous improvement is being thoroughly embraced. However, we realize how difficult such a transition can be, especially given the growing pressures on governments to produce more results with fewer resources. Therefore, our goal for this guide is for you to *ask the right questions*. Here are a few examples that illustrate why asking the right questions from a "benchmarking mind-set" can be so powerful.

Example 1: If the local historical society asks your town board for a budget increase, you should immediately request some basic information. This includes the number of visitors, the overall budget balance and the procedures used to estimate costs, as well as the goals that will be achieved if the budget is increased.

Example 2: If the assessor asks to hire more clerical staff, you should ask for per parcel costs and how this compares to assessment offices in similar towns in the vicinity.

Example 3: If you are considering merit raises for department heads, you should ask: Is a customer survey conducted on a regular basis and, if so, what are the results?

These examples do not use the word benchmark, but its spirit is clearly evident. We encourage you to embrace this spirit, even if you do not use the actual term.

Main Points

✓ Benchmarking will put your government firmly on the road to continuous improvement.

✓ Indicators + Goals = Benchmarks.

✓ Benchmarking can help contain costs, increase workloads, improve efficiency, enhance the quality of government service and lead to a better quality of life.

✓ Benchmarking is grounded in the specific.

Chapter 12

Two Basic Building Blocks

Learn About

✓ **How to determine your benchmarking goals**

✓ **The advantages and disadvantages of different methods of goal setting**

✓ **Collecting information about the goals you have set**

✓ **Obstacles to getting all the necessary information**

Benchmarking requires a mind-set that forces you to continually ask:

Goals: What are we trying to accomplish?

Measurement: How will we know if we have done it?

Such a mind-set should shape your thinking about the performance of government, just as it should shape all kinds of decisions in other aspects of your life. Identifying goals and checking for progress is the hallmark of a stellar elected official.

These two questions are the building blocks of all benchmarking. If you cannot answer them, you cannot benchmark. If you can, you are ready and able to improve the performance of your government.

Block #1: Choosing Goals

Identifying and agreeing upon goals might seem difficult, but only if you are a perfectionist. A more relaxed approach toward these goals will yield better results. Think of your goals as approximations you can adjust if they do not prove helpful. Initially the "correct" goal may elude you. Therefore, it is important to start the process and to continuously modify the goals as more information becomes available.

We have some easy guidelines to follow, as well as a chart to show you how to choose those goals.

Three Ways to Set Goals

Method of Analysis	Description	Police Example
Absolute Analysis	You have a level in mind.	95% of citizens say they feel safe when walking at night.
Analysis Over Time	You want to be better than last year.	Reduce the annual number of violent crimes by 10%.
Comparative Analysis	You want to be better than average.	Clear more cases than the county average.

You can use one or more of these methods to choose goals as your benchmarks. You may use a combination. Different approaches may be more appropriate at different times. Each method has both advantages and disadvantages.

Optional

The next three pages explain each of the three methods in more detail, outlining the pros and cons. If you are not ready for this discussion, go to page 78 to learn about the second building block.

1. The Absolute Level Method

Choosing an *absolute level* can be arbitrary and, if you choose the highest level, it may be so far out of reach that it threatens credibility and defeats the purpose of using benchmarks. However, absolute levels have their place. For example, a benchmark for the local police department might be to gain state accreditation. By deciding that accreditation is important, you have identified an absolute benchmark and, if the majority of police departments in your county are accredited, it is reasonable to assume that all should be accredited.

Absolute levels can be based on arbitrary selection such as "the literacy rate for the United States should be 100 percent." But the best approach is to have these levels come from an authoritative government or professional agency, as in the police accreditation example. The problem is that there are not enough standards for many government services. Moreover, many standards are open to serious question, because special interests may shape them. For example, until recently some considered New York State educational standards too low because educators wanted high success rates. Now some argue that they are too high because some educators and their political supporters want to look "tough."

> ## Pros and Cons of the Absolute Level Method
>
> **Pros:** Easy to understand and measure.
>
> **Cons:** Open to questions of credibility driven by concerns of vested interests leading to standards that are too high or too low; tend to be simplistic.

As you read in Chapter 1, our favorite absolute level benchmark for many government services is the use of customer surveys. This standard has the advantage of being easy to determine. Either the department does or does not conduct customer surveys. The disadvantage is that the requirement is simplistic, since it assumes that the procedure is not biased and that the department heads actually use the results. To deal with these concerns, more complicated standards would have to be developed and applied, including giving the results to elected officials on a routine basis and reporting the information to the public.

2. The Analysis Over Time Method

Choosing the analysis over time method makes a lot of sense in many cases. You can plot an indicator such as the response time to police calls for three to five years. If the department's performance is deteriorating, you simply choose the benchmark to raise it to the best year. If you are concerned about complaints in the assessor's office, you can call for a percentage reduction in the number of complaints from the previous year. Setting benchmarks that call for some level of improvement works in many cases. However if performance is very low, calling for some percentage increase may still leave a government service behind by creating a benchmark that lets everyone off the hook.

> ## Pros and Cons of the Analysis Over Time Method
>
> **Pros:** More credible than the absolute method and less costly than the comparative method; easy to reach consensus on goal.
>
> **Cons:** Beginning at a low level tends to produce low benchmarks.

This method is more powerful than the absolute standard method because it is more credible. The existing performance is known and the direction it should move is clear. The only threat to credibility is controversy over how much improvement to seek. An easy way to deal with such disagreement is to split the difference.

3. The Comparative Method

The comparative method is usually conducive to analysis over time. The average performance of all municipalities in the county, for example, can be used as the basis for the benchmark. You may want to be above average, but you still use the average as the source of measurement. Comparing across several units allows for ranking, which can lead to a benchmark such as being in the top three for a county. This way of using rankings creates an easily understood benchmark.

While rankings often drive the point home, there is a downside. Rankings force artificial competition and can backfire. This is especially true if there isn't much variation in performance. Your municipality may have the lowest ranking, but only by a difference of two percent when compared to the top municipality. Thus, spending more money to be on top may not be useful. For this reason, using the average as the benchmark is generally preferable to ranking.

Pros and Cons of the Comparative Method

 Pros: Most credible way to set goals; rankings gain attention.

 Cons: Costly to collect; danger of making insignificant comparisons; rankings can backfire.

The big disadvantage of the comparative approach is that it is time-consuming and costly to compile the information. If you are studying your town compared with five or more other towns, you have to collect data on those other towns. Without that data you cannot find the average. Getting the data can be difficult because local governments do not necessarily keep good records. Before you choose the comparative method, you should talk to your counterparts in other towns to see what kind of data is available. You could also approach county officials to find out if they have the resources to collect and analyze the data.

Moreover, the use of comparison assumes that your municipality is similar to the other municipalities used for the comparison. Municipalities with a lower per capita income will usually look worse compared with those with richer populations. For example, rich communities generally have lower violent crime rates than poor communities. You will need to take this into account when interpreting your rankings.

Block #2: Getting Information   END OF SIDE TRIP

Once you've defined the service you want to measure, you will have to determine if the information is readily available or if you will have to collect the data. Sometimes you can use past government records, such as examining a sample of code violation reports; other times you may need to conduct a survey. Surveys can range in complexity from a simple customer survey citizens complete when they visit a government office to a random telephone survey of the general population. In some cases, you will need the cooperation of several government departments to collect information from these records or to conduct surveys.

You will know how much information to collect by the goal you select. If you use an absolute method for selecting the goal, you only need to acquire information for the current time period. If you use the analysis over time method, you will need information for at least the current and previous years. If you use the comparative method, you need to get information for all the units in your sample.

Chapters 13 through 17 show how to collect the information you will need to use benchmarks.

Now the Bad News About Getting and Using Information

Unfortunately, getting precise information on indicators is the most difficult, time-consuming and frustrating part of benchmarking. Reliable, comparable and accurate information is difficult to obtain for a number of reasons, including:

- *Major complications in analysis.* Creating useful indicators requires expertise and serious attention to detail.
- *Difficulty in obtaining data.* Few workers and managers rank "keeping data on a systematic basis" as a very high priority.
- *Difficulty in making comparisons.* Governments collect indicators in different ways and for different time periods.
- *"Lies, damn lies and statistics."* Small changes in the way indicators are collected and displayed can produce very different results.

Coming up with good measures that show accurate data can be tricky. Even cost figures may be difficult to get because not all budgets are organized by the specific functions being measured. The measures themselves may appear to indicate one thing but relate to something different. For example, the number of DWI arrests may be an indicator of good police work or an indicator of the inability of the police and their officials to educate the public. If it is the first indicator, then the higher the number of arrests, the better. If it is the second indicator, then the lower the number of arrests, the better. Only knowledge and careful thought will yield meaningful and helpful benchmarks.

> **"Lies, damn lies and statistics."**
> **–Mark Twain**

The bad news also extends to the actual use of numbers such as percentages, rates and trend graphs as suggested by the Mark Twain quote. The book, *How to Lie with Statistics*[1] alerts you to the way in which numbers can be manipulated to make the point you want to make. The increasing use of scorecarding, which we discuss in Chapter 18, has raised the stakes in the art of manipulating numbers. Space does not permit us to provide you with all the protection you need, considering all the potential pitfalls of using numbers. The best advice we can provide is to review your charts and graphs with others to make sure you can defend them.

---

[1] Huff, Darrel with Irving Geis (illustrator). *How to Lie With Statistics*. 1993.

Main Points

✓ **Always focus on:**

What am I trying to accomplish?

How will I know when I succeed?

✓ **Three methods of choosing goals are Absolute, Annual and Comparative.**

✓ **Comparative is best, but the other two are useful.**

✓ **Getting information can be time consuming, but is critical.**

Chapter 13
Benchmarking the Costs of Government Services

Learn About

✓ Easy to use benchmarking formats
✓ Use of cost indicators
✓ How to choose cost goals
✓ Sources of cost information
✓ Steps for benchmarking the costs of government services

We start with the costs of government services because money gets everybody's attention. Spending also carries an implicit goal: *Reduce it as much as possible!*

However, costs are only a small piece of the benchmarking puzzle. We will describe the rest of the pieces in subsequent chapters. These puzzle pieces include:

◆ How much work results from each dollar spent
◆ How competently the work is done
◆ The impact of government services on society

Benchmarking the Costs of Police Services

Government officials are constantly under pressure to reduce costs. For example, citizens may claim that too many of their tax dollars go to the local police department. Benchmarking can help you respond by communicating your goals for government expenditure.

Jargon Protection

The term "input" is a word professional researchers use to describe the resources allocated to provide a specific service. We use the term "cost" to mean the same thing because it is more easily understood. Cost is usually measured in dollars but could also be expressed in staff hours.

This chapter shows you how to start making judgments by looking at costs. In the subsequent chapters we show you how to consider this assessment in conjunction with workload, efficiency, quality and your results.

In the previous chapter, we introduced the three ways of setting goals for benchmarks: absolute standards, analysis over time and comparative analysis. When examining costs, however, absolute standards are not very useful. Since there are very few, if any, generally accepted levels of spending, absolute standards cannot help to answer your questions.

We show you how to conduct analysis over time and comparative analysis in this chapter. We also introduce formats we have found effective in presenting our benchmarks to the community and government officials. You may copy the formats we provide and adapt them as you wish. The information is designed only to get you started on the road to benchmarking government costs. Once you start down that road, you will be able to anticipate sharp curves, dead ends and roadblocks in helping your government control costs and making wise allocations.

1. Analysis Over Time

This method is the easiest to understand. It simply asks, "What would you like your expenditures to be next year, compared with this one?" The most frequent basis of choice for your benchmark is the current year plus inflation. This analysis is described in the case study on the next page.

This case study also introduces you to the trials and tribulations of using numbers. Numbers can be your friends or your enemies, so, in using benchmarks, you must use them with as much care as when balancing your checkbook. The best way to deal with people who challenge you on number-cruncher questions is to be prepared. Start by acknowledging that the challenger may be right. If the number crunchers have a valid point, adjust your benchmark accordingly.

The case study below illustrates the analysis over time approach for a cost study. Clearly Town A exceeds the benchmark

Case Study: Analysis Over Time of Police Expenditures Per Capita

Town A has a per capita expenditure for its police services of $75.13 in 2000. The town council has established as a general guideline that no department should spend more than its current level of spending, plus inflation. Assuming inflation is 2.5% in 2000, the benchmark for the year 2001 would be $77.01. After 2001 expenditures are known it is possible to determine whether or not the Town met its benchmark and by how much.

Armed with this data, you will be able to demonstrate in the year 2002 that the police department's per capita expenditures in 2001 were more than they were in 2000 plus inflation. This finding allows you to conclude that police costs may be increasing too much.

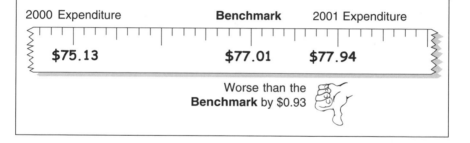

2000 Expenditure	**Benchmark**	2001 Expenditure
$75.13	**$77.01**	**$77.94**

Worse than the
Benchmark by $0.93

This case study raises a question that you will always need to ask: Does the two-year comparison make sense or should you look at a longer time period? What would we conclude if the 1999 per capita expenditure had been $77 and the 2000 figure of $75.13 was the lowest it had been in five years? We would have probably set a higher benchmark. For this reason, it is preferable to use an average of the previous five to 10 years before setting a benchmark for the next year by using the previous year as a base.

There are many other potential problems, such as the accuracy of the budget figures and whether expenditures were higher because of new programs funded by outside sources. These kinds of questions cannot be avoided, and they may cause you to give up the whole exercise. However, the use of simple quantitative numbers in a benchmarking format is better than the alternative of arguing over whether expenditures are too high without a clear foundation from which to make a judgment.

2. Comparative Analysis

The analysis over time approach is a good start, but it does not answer the question of how Town A compares to other towns. For that reason, it is usually a good idea to use data comparing your municipality with similar municipalities (if you have access to those figures), as we have done in the next case study.

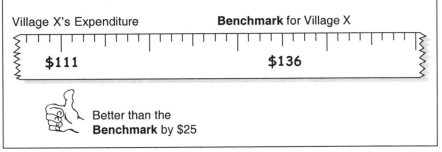

Case Study: Comparative Benchmark of Police Expenditures Per Capita

We could set a benchmark for Village X's police department per capita expenditures by looking at the average of the other villages in the county. There are five other police departments that we can use to get the average. Village X would want their per capita expenditures to be no more than the average benchmark. We can see if Village X meets the benchmark for a past year by looking at the ruler graphic below.

Village X's Expenditure   **Benchmark** for Village X

$111 $136

Better than the
Benchmark by $25

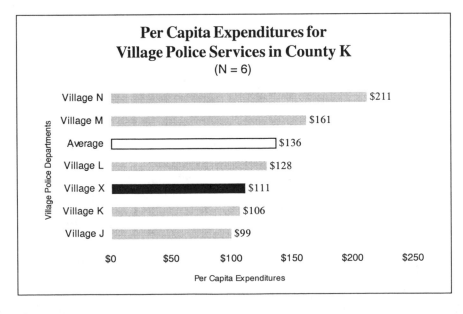

Per Capita Expenditures for Village Police Services in County K
(N = 6)

- Village N — $211
- Village M — $161
- Average — $136
- Village L — $128
- Village X — $111
- Village K — $106
- Village J — $99

Village Police Departments

$0 $50 $100 $150 $200 $250

Per Capita Expenditures

Providing more information related to the comparative benchmark can drive the results home. The chart on the previous page shows per capita expenditures for all six villages. Village X is the third lowest.

This would be a happy benchmarking result if you were the mayor of Village X since you would be doing better than average. But wait! Not so fast! Look at the Number Cruncher Protector below to understand the complexities of choosing units to make comparisons.

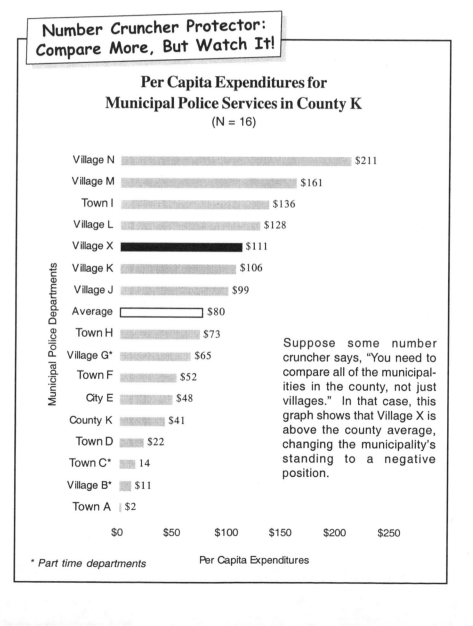

Number Cruncher Protector: Compare More, But Watch It!

Per Capita Expenditures for Municipal Police Services in County K
(N = 16)

Municipal Police Departments

Municipality	Per Capita Expenditures
Village N	$211
Village M	$161
Town I	$136
Village L	$128
Village X	$111
Village K	$106
Village J	$99
Average	$80
Town H	$73
Village G*	$65
Town F	$52
City E	$48
County K	$41
Town D	$22
Town C*	14
Village B*	$11
Town A	$2

$0 $50 $100 $150 $200 $250

Per Capita Expenditures

* Part time departments

Suppose some number cruncher says, "You need to compare all of the municipalities in the county, not just villages." In that case, this graph shows that Village X is above the county average, changing the municipality's standing to a negative position.

Budgets as Sources of Cost Indicators

Most cost information will come from your municipal budget. This is sufficient for analysis over time studies, but you will gain more information through comparative studies with other municipalities. States and counties may compile comparative financial data for local municipalities that can be useful. The availability of this data varies and often is outdated. To obtain information on budgets from other municipalities, you will most likely have to contact your counterparts in other communities to request their budget information. If you explain the goal of your project, they may see the benefit of having the comparative information for their own use. Once you have collected the data, it will be necessary to normalize your findings in order to make accurate comparisons. Refer to the following Number Cruncher Protector for information on per capita as well as how to normalize your findings.

Number Cruncher Protector: The Importance of Per Capita

By using the per capita amount rather than total expenditures, we can compare Town X to bigger or smaller towns. Per capita amounts are easily calculated by dividing whatever you're looking at (e.g., total expenditures) by the population size.

The use of per capita raises a general point about the need to use population and other types of descriptive variables (e.g., land area or number of households) in some cost studies. You will usually need to do what the number crunchers call "normalize" your findings. Normalizing means to scale the numbers so that they can be more easily compared. Your choice can be critical! For example, per capita police expenditures may penalize departments that have a large geographic area to cover. This is especially important if you use comparative analysis. Another thing to watch out for is the use of per capita. This is explained in the Number Cruncher Protector on pages 92.

Steps for Benchmarking Government Service Costs

Step 1: Select a government service for which cost is an issue.

Step 2: Decide whether to use analysis over time or comparative analysis.

Step 3: Collect the appropriate data. For analysis over time, you need data on your town for different time periods. For comparative analysis, you need data from at least four towns in the county for the most recent year. You may want to average data for the past three years to account for uneven patterns.

Step 4: Look carefully at your data and charts. If you see that costs have gone up more than inflation or that they are higher than costs in other comparable towns, you might want to publicize the study in presentations to other officials, government managers and the public. Think about the Number Cruncher Protector on pages 84 and 85.

Step 5: Decide which format you want to use in public discussions and written presentations. You may choose to keep the comparative information in the back of your mind. Benchmarking is a way of thinking first and then a way of presenting.

Step 6: Understand that cost information alone is not sufficient. You must also consider the departmental workload, the quality of government service and impact on the community. For that, read the next chapters and then return to the question of costs.

Main Points

✓ Costs are a good place to start, but are only a beginning.

✓ Comparing one year with the next is a good start, but a trend of five to 10 years is better.

✓ Compare at least four, but preferably all, municipalities with similar characteristics.

✓ Cost data is frequently difficult to obtain because of the different ways it is reported. Budgets will be your key source of information.

✓ Follow the steps for benchmarking the costs of services.

Chapter 14

Benchmarking the Workload of Government Services

Learn About

✓ **Ways to benchmark the amount of work governments do**

✓ **Sources of workload indicators**

✓ **Ways to request information**

✓ **Steps for benchmarking government service workloads**

Benchmarking costs are only a beginning because taxpayers are frequently willing to pay more for better schools, roads or police services. In fact, looking only at costs can be dangerous to the survival of an elected official. Reducing a highly valued service as part of a cost-saving effort may end a political career.

Consequently, costs based on the amount of work a department does are better than simple cost or workload information. You can use cost and workload information to study the efficiency of government services, such as how much it costs for each service provided. This chapter shows you how to collect and present information on benchmarking the workload of government services. The next chapter will show you how to put cost and workload together to measure efficiency of government services.

Jargon Protection

Professional researchers use the term "output" to describe the activities of a government agency. The term "workload measure" indicates how many services are provided in any given number of instances. We use the term "workload of government services" to indicate the same thing. The language is awkward, but hopefully it reduces confusion and sounds less like jargon than "output."

Benchmarking the Workload of the Police Department

In the previous chapter we saw how to find out whether your police department costs more than others in the county. But how do we assess a police department's workload? We can use the analysis over time method as well as the comparative analysis method to explore this question.

1. Analysis Over Time

As noted in Chapter 12, this method only requires data collection from one municipality and therefore, is the easiest route. Take a look at the following case study to see how the analysis over time method can be used in benchmarking the workload of the police department in a municipality.

Case Study: Benchmark of Village X's Average Number of Patrol Units Over Time

If you are concerned with the increasing crime rate in your municipality, you may want your police chief to send more uniformed police to the streets. A suitable benchmark would be to increase the average number of patrol units on the street between midnight and 8 a.m. by 10 percent from the previous year. The following ruler depicts data for Village X for the years 1995 and 1996.

As you can see in the ruler graphic below, the police department did not meet the workload benchmark.

If you want to see if the long-term pattern is different from the years you have chosen, you should construct a 10-year trend line graph.

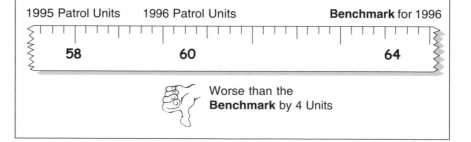

1995 Patrol Units   1996 Patrol Units   **Benchmark** for 1996

58   60   64

Worse than the **Benchmark** by 4 Units

2.Comparative Analysis

This method of analysis is often more useful than analysis over time when dealing with workloads. It makes more sense to compare one department with others, rather than simply to compare a department with itself over time.

The case study below compares the workload of one village police department with the county average.

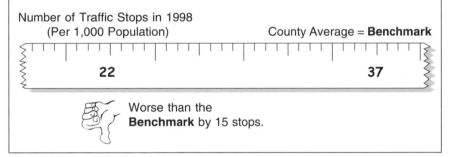

Case Study: Comparative Benchmark of Village X's Annual Number of Vehicle and Traffic Stops

You might use this type of analysis when you want to show that a department is doing more than other departments. For example, if a department wants to reduce speeding in the village, it might spend more time than other departments making vehicle and traffic stops. A suitable benchmark would be to have at least as many vehicle and traffic stops as the county average for all full-time village police departments.

Number of Traffic Stops in 1998
(Per 1,000 Population)   County Average = **Benchmark**

22   37

Worse than the
Benchmark by 15 stops.

The information in the format used or the case study provides a limited perspective. The bar graph on the opposite page shows that not only did the village not meet the benchmark, it ranked poorly in contrast to other villages.

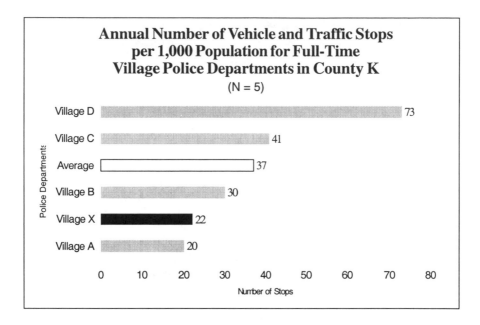

Annual Number of Vehicle and Traffic Stops per 1,000 Population for Full-Time Village Police Departments in County K

(N = 5)

Police Department	Number of Stops
Village D	73
Village C	41
Average	37
Village B	30
Village X	22
Village A	20

Number of Stops

Number Cruncher Protector: When to Use Rates Instead of Per Capita

You may need something other than per capita even if you want to relate workload to population size. You might find that when you use per capita amounts, you get really small numbers (i.e., less than 1). This usually happens when you have a large population and a small number of observations. One way of making the data easier to read is to multiply the per capita amount by 1,000, 10,000 or some other number. For example, if you multiply the per capita amount by 1,000, you find the number of observances for every 1,000 residents. Thus, the following formula may be used:

Per Capita Amount = (Number of Observations/Population) X 1,000

One of the most popular uses of this technique is the FBI's crime rate statistics. Since the crime rate is so small on the per capita basis (e.g., Denver's is 0.06647), the FBI reports the crime rate as crimes per 100,000 population. Thus, the crime rate becomes 6,647 per 100,000 population.

For helpful information about using per capita amounts see the Number Cruncher Protector on page 86.

Sources of Workload Indicators

Government documents that record the activities of most government agencies are the primary source of workload indicators. Government publications that go to the public or other government units such as the county, state or federal government can contain significant amounts of information. The table below presents some workload measures for different government operations.

Examples of Workload Indicators for Other Government Services

Although there is more information available on police activity than many other government services, workload information can be found for many areas. This is illustrated in the following table.

Function	Workload Description
Police	Annual number of police calls
Fire, Rescue & Emergency Services	Annual number of fire and EMS calls
Parks & Recreation	Acres of parkland maintained
Courts	Annual number of cases heard
Trash Collection	Annual tons of trash collected
Water Department	Annual number of meters repaired
Building & Code Enforcement	Annual number of construction inspections
Library	Annual circulation
Planning Department	Annual number of land use reviews conducted

There are two types of workload information: quantity of services delivered and range of services. Although this chapter has primarily covered the quantity of services delivered, the range of services should be considered in some cases.

Trash collection is a good example. If your constituents pay the same price as residents in another municipality, they would expect the same level of service. For example, if the other municipality collects trash at the garage, your constituents would want the same service.

Service Description	Village X	Village Y
Costs per Capita	$174	$175
Collects White Goods	Yes	No
Collects Yard Debris	Yes	Yes
Collects Tires	Yes	No
Collects Batteries	Yes	No
Collects Construction Debris	Yes	Yes

One study by the Community Benchmarks Program revealed vast differences in the range of services provided. Most often, the simplest way to present the information is in a table. For example, two munici-palities that charge about the same amount for trash collection may provide vastly different services.

Displaying the range of services may allow you to explain why your costs or expenditures are high compared with others. You could also establish as a benchmark that all services be provided.

Steps for Benchmarking the Workload of Government Services

Step 1: Choose a workload measure based on one of the following criteria:
- It is related to your concern about cost that you may have already benchmarked.
- You think the department may be doing either too much or too little of something, or you may want to use the information as a point of reference.

Step 2: Decide whether to use analysis over time or comparative analysis.

Step 3: Collect appropriate data.

Step 4: Look carefully at your data and charts and think about whether the information supports your original view. If the evidence suggests there has been a decline in the number of patrol units and your constituents feel that crime has gotten worse, you could use this type of information to support an increase in patrol units.

Step 5: Decide which of the two formats – analysis over time or comparative analysis – you want to use in public discussions and written presen-tations. You may keep the information in the back of your mind.

Step 6: Understand that workload information alone is not sufficient. If you are going to relate workload information to costs and quality, you need to combine it with analysis as described in the previous chapter and the next chapter. If you are going to relate it to the percent of effort of the department, you must collect other workload data and use comparisons to suggest how priorities may be readjusted.

You must also consider the cost of providing the services, the quality of the services and their impact on the community. For that, you need to learn what is presented in Chapters 15 through 17 and then return to your assessment of workload information.

Main Points

✓ **Workload includes both the amount and the range of services.**

✓ **Analysis over time of workload is much easier to use than comparative analysis.**

✓ **Comparative analysis of workload is more useful than analysis over time.**

✓ **Government records are a primary source of workload information.**

Chapter 15

Benchmarking the Efficiency of Government Services

Benchmarking the Efficiency of Police Services

In the previous two chapters, you learned how to measure cost and workload. In this chapter, we show you how to connect the two types of indicators. By doing so, you will be able to measure the efficiency, or the cost per unit provided. This chapter helps you answer the question: *How much does each unit of service cost and is this cost a good value?*

To answer this, you need both cost information (annual police expenditures is a good start) and workload information (such as total number of incidents). With these numbers, you can find the average expense per incident by dividing the total expenditures by the number of incidents.

Workload costs usually represent efficiency, which tells you if the department has a workload appropriate to its expenditures. Knowing this can help control costs, but it is not the final step to benchmarking for better government. You also want to know the quality of police services and the impact it has on crime. These two aspects will be presented in Chapters 16 and 17.

1. Analysis Over Time

Case Study: Benchmark Over Time of Town X's Expenditure per Reported Crime

We will look at average expenditures on reported crimes over time to give you an idea of what an efficiency indicator looks like using this method. An appropriate benchmark is to have the yearly increase in the expense per reported crime remain below the increase in inflation.

Town X did not meet this benchmark for 2001 when compared with 2000. However, you should also look at the pattern over a 10-year period to see if your choice of benchmarks makes sense.

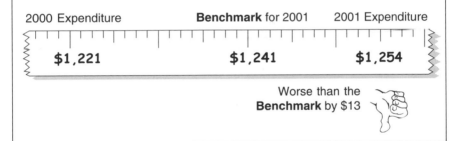

2000 Expenditure	**Benchmark** for 2001	2001 Expenditure
$1,221	$1,241	$1,254

Worse than the
Benchmark by $13

2. Comparative Analysis

Comparative analysis for efficiency is more powerful than analysis over time. In the next case study, we examine average expense per police incident for all full-time town police departments in County K. As is usual when doing comparative analysis, we set our benchmark as the average. We are happy if we are below the mean, or average, expense per incident in the county.

The comparison graph on the next page is a good way to display relative efficiency of town police departments. Residents in Town X would likely want to know why their cost per incident is so high and how other departments keep their cost per incident low.

When doing efficiency studies, keep in mind that there are often reasons behind a department's perceived inefficiency. For example, Town X may have a high cost per incident because they have few incidents and spend a lot of money on prevention. Thus the total amount spent on police may be similar to other departments, but the allocation may reduce the number of incidents. You could check this by

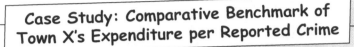

Case Study: Comparative Benchmark of Town X's Expenditure per Reported Crime

Residents in Town X should not be pleased with these results. The police department not only failed to meet the benchmark but missed it by almost $100 per incident! If you wanted to provide more detail, you might create a graph like the one in the next box to show how poorly the department performed compared to others in the county. This finding could help elect a candidate for the town council who criticized the efficiency of the police department. A defender of the status quo would be in serious trouble if this were a concern of the electorate.

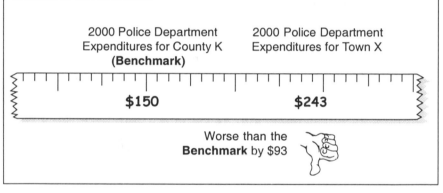

2000 Police Department Expenditures for County K **(Benchmark)**

2000 Police Department Expenditures for Town X

$150

$243

Worse than the **Benchmark** by $93

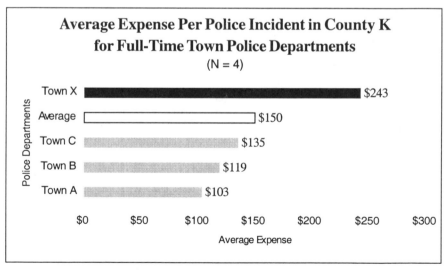

Average Expense Per Police Incident in County K for Full-Time Town Police Departments
(N = 4)

Police Departments

Town X — $243
Average — $150
Town C — $135
Town B — $119
Town A — $103

$0 $50 $100 $150 $200 $250 $300

Average Expense

looking at total cost per capita. If Town X is high in this area, then its efficiency is presumably low. However, if total cost per capita is low, the high cost per incident may not be a problem.

Number Cruncher Protector:
Other Costs per Workload Measures

In addition to relating cost and workload, another very effective way to measure efficiency is by looking at the workload per FTE (full-time equivalent) employee. FTE is preferable to employee, because FTE allows you to make equivalent comparisons between departments with staff that work full time, part time or a combination of both. By using FTE, two employees who each work 20 hours a week will be equivalent to one full-time staff member.

The workload per FTE employee lets you see if the department is overstaffed, understaffed or just right. An example of this type of analysis is the number of reported crimes per FTE law enforcement employee.

Steps for Benchmarking the Efficiency of Government Services

Step 1: Find a government service about which you or your constituents want to know the value of the work performed.

Step 2: Decide whether to use analysis over time or comparative analysis.

Step 3: Collect appropriate data using Chapters 12 and 13 as a guideline.

Step 4: Carefully review the data and charts. In our previous examples regarding the average expense per police incident in County K, the evidence suggests that some departments (e.g., Town X at $243 per incident) may need to look at why their costs are so high compared to the amount of work they do. With an average expense that is slightly less than double the county average, Town X police department may have something to learn from more efficient departments such as in towns B and C. If nothing else, information similar to that displayed in the chart should stimulate communication between departments.

Step 5: Decide which of the two formats – analysis over time or comparative analysis – will be the most useful. You may choose to use them for your own analysis or to present them publicly.

Step 6: Recognize that efficiency information alone is not sufficient. You must also consider the quality of services and the impact on the community. For that, you need to read Chapters 16 and 17.

Benchmarking Efficiency Measures for Other Government Services

The chart below lists a few of the more obvious cost per unit measures for assessing the efficiency of local government services. Information sources for these areas would be the same as those suggested in Chapters 13 and 14 for acquiring data on costs and workloads.

Examples of Efficiency Measures for Other Government Services

Function	Efficiency Indicator
Police	Average cost per incident
Fire, Rescue & Emergency Services	Annual number of fire and medical incidents per on-duty emergency staff
Parks & Recreation	Average cost of maintaining one developed park acre
Transportation	Annual maintenance cost per lane mile
Trash Collection & Disposal	Average weekly tons collected per FTE (full-time equivalent) trash collection employee
Water Supply	Average cost of new water mains installed per foot
Buildings	Number of building inspections per FTE employee
Housing & Community Development	Average cost of minor rehabilitation on low to moderate income homeowner units
Planning	Number of permit applications per FTE employee

Main Points

✓ **Efficiency can be defined as a ratio of cost to workload.**

✓ **Knowledge of government services and costs is crucial to developing good efficiency measures.**

✓ **Knowledge of outside factors is critical to reaching conclusions about efficiency.**

Chapter 16

Benchmarking the Quality of Government Services

Ben & Jerry's ice cream costs more than generic brands, but that does not prevent its sale to those who value its taste enough to pay for it. Therefore, in addition to setting benchmarks for the cost adjusted for workload, you must determine the quality of those services.

But how do we measure quality? The answer can be found in the way business leaders assess the quality of their products and services. They do this in three ways:

♦ Company records that provide such information as the number of defects per 1,000 units or the durability of the product.

♦ Customer surveys that ask customers to assess products and services.

♦ Quality assurance standards established by professional associations and both governmental and non-governmental accreditation agencies.

Each approach has also been used in assessing quality of government services. In this chapter, we will briefly describe the first two. Quality assurance standards were addressed in our discussion of the bare essentials of government presented in Part One.

Government Records

In many cases, government records can be an important component for measuring the quality of government services. For example, you may want to know how quickly your police department responds to high priority calls. The information won't be found by surveying users or employees. It can only be found by looking at government records. Therefore, high-priority response time is one of the most frequently used indicators of the quality of a department's service. Clearly, a good department will respond to an emergency quickly. Government records can be used for any type of service. The table below provides some examples.

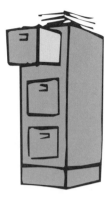

Examples of Quality Indicators for Other Government Services

Function	Quality Indicator
Police	Percent of all cases cleared
Fire, Rescue & Emergency Services	Emergency medical services average response time
Parks and Recreation	Percent of equipment in good working order
Transportation	Percent of potholes repaired within 48 hours of notification
Trash Collection & Disposal	Annual number of formal complaints per 1,000 population
Water Supply	Percent of positive samples with coloform bacteria
Building Codes	Percent of buildings inspected for fire hazards annually
Property Assessments	Ratio of appraised value to an independent estimate of market value, such as sale price

In these examples, all three approaches to benchmarking – absolute analysis, analysis over time and comparative analysis – can be used. Absolute standards can be set by higher government agencies. For example, the state could require that all towns inspect 100 percent of commercial buildings for compliance with fire safety regulation each year. Analysis over time could be set by calling for a 10 percent reduction in complaints about trash collection. The ratio of appraised to market value of property assessment could be compared with other towns in the area. Consequently, the three formats presented in other chapters could be used to display whether or not your town met the benchmark.

Customer Surveys

 By far the most valuable approach to assessing the quality of a government service is to ask recent users to comment on the quality of service. You will find this item on almost every Bare Essential Checklist in Part One. Customer surveys provide ideas about how to improve services. Benchmarking is about continuous improvement, so suggestions from citizens should be built into your effort.

For example, the response of police to a homeowner who heard a suspicious noise late at night can be assessed through a follow-up mail survey to the caller. The survey could ask the respondent to comment on how prompt, courteous and thorough the police were. In addition, the respondent can be asked what the police might have done differently. Appendix A provides a format for effective customer surveys appropriate for a variety of services.

The most feasible method of analysis for customer surveys is analysis over time. To set an absolute level, such as the office should score a 10 (using a 1-10 scale) across all citizen responses is probably unrealistic. More practical might be to consider an eight or higher as the benchmark staff should strive to reach.

Once you collect the results, what you do with the information is important. Generally, all departments that provide direct service should use customer surveys and the findings should be reported to elected officials, the respective department head, and his or her staff. Release of the survey results to the public may be met with resistance from staff, but it may also serve as a catalyst for continuous improvement. The existence of Freedom of Information laws in many states may require this action.

There is a secondary reason for conducting customer surveys on a systematic basis. Given the growing sophistication of citizens, customer surveys can help your government avoid problems by anticipating them. There is often a concern that certain services may evoke negative responses, such as the office of property assessment. We

A Note About Surveys

A customer survey is *not* a general survey of the entire population. It is a survey of people who have used the service recently and of those who can make very specific comments on the quality of that service. Someone surveyed 48 hours after being stopped by the police for a traffic violation could participate in a customer survey. Asking a sample of the people living in a town what they think about police services is a general population survey, which is less effective in improving services than a customer survey. Appendix A shows how general surveys can help to assess the quality of life in the community. To evaluate government services, customer surveys are preferred.

believe that most citizens are able to differentiate between being displeased with the assessed value assigned to their property and whether the staff is responsive to their concerns, they have been treated courteously or they are given all the information necessary to file an appeal. Those occasions when respondents are unable to separate quality service from a result they do not agree with are usually balanced by the number of people who can make this distinction. Negative responses need only be a concern when a large percent of the responses are negative, which indicates a problem in the department. The occasionally disapproving response may come from a contrary customer who can never be pleased, or perhaps the staff person was having a rare "bad day." Giving citizens a voice by providing an opportunity for feedback will improve both the image of the department and of the elected officials in the eyes of the public.

Appendix A provides you with a step-by-step guide to create your own customer survey, as well as a generic customer survey form that you can adapt to your needs. If you take the time to create a draft survey and form a guideline for collecting information, the results will prove valuable. As an elected official, you should require the use of customer surveys to help you be better attuned to the needs of the electorate and the quality of service municipal employees provide.

Benchmarking the Quality of Government Services

Step 1: Find a government service you feel requires a quality study.

Step 2: Decide which indicators you want to use:

     ◆   Government Records

     ◆   Customer Surveys

Step 3: Collect the appropriate data using this chapter as a guideline. If a customer survey is not already used on a regular basis, ask to have one developed and implemented. This is usually the best place to start. Examine Chapters 13 though 17 which explain how you can use government records and quality assurance standards to improve the quality of government services.

Step 4: If you think that a department needs to improve the quality of its service, look carefully at your data and charts. Determine if you have support for your conclusion. Check with surrounding towns to see if you can get advice on the standards that would be most useful to reach. Contact the professional associations identified in Chapters 2 through 10.

Step 5: Understand that the quality of service must also be connected to the cost of service and to the overall impact on the community's goals. You may want your police department to meet the national standards set for the best departments, but you may not want to spend the money to make the necessary changes.

Main Points

✓ Quality of government services is difficult to measure. It requires different approaches to collecting information than those used for cost or workload measurement.

✓ Some government records provide information on quality of services, but rarely provide enough information to measure quality of services comprehensively.

✓ Customer surveys are powerful tools that help to improve a department by identifying the source of the problems.

Chapter 17

Benchmarking the Quality of Life in Your Community

Learn About

✓ Why quality of life measures are critical to your success

✓ How to use general population surveys, government records and direct observation to measure the quality of life in your community

✓ Avoiding the dangers associated with quality of life studies

✓ Steps for benchmarking the quality of life in your community

If concerns only focused on the efficiency and quality of government services, governance would be somewhat easier. The reality is that some of the most pressing issues are connected to a community's quality of life. While a broad range of issues exists under this umbrella, they tend to boil down to whether the environment is healthy, pleasant and safe. Benchmarking can be key in the never-ending pursuit of making a community better.

Collecting information on quality of life indicators is more costly, time-consuming and subject to data problems than benchmarking cost, workload, efficiency and quality of specific government services. Quality of life indicators frequently require data local governments do not keep. For that reason, we recommend you undertake benchmarking quality of life only after you have had some experience using benchmarking for government services and that you see it primarily as a way to promote community problem-solving.

Quality of Life as a Process in Community Problem Solving

Benchmarking to help raise the quality of life in your community requires you to understand the limited role of government in that pursuit. Quality of life indicators are only partially affected by what governments do. The behavior and attitude of the entire community, its physical setting and outside forces such as the national economy play the overriding role. People who drop their trash on the ground, for example, are going to leave dirty streets regardless of the quality of trash service.

Because government has a limited role in improving the community, benchmarking should be viewed as a mechanism for getting everyone responsible for the problems in the community to work together. This means building a coalition among government officials, not-for-profit institutions, private business and citizens with the purpose of recognizing a problem and agreeing on how each will work to help solve it. As an elected official, you can help by gaining agreement on how best to measure the problem or condition and by stimulating discussions on what needs to be done.

Jargon Protection

Professional researchers use the term "effectiveness" to describe government services that accomplish what they are supposed to be doing. Be careful not to confuse this word with the word "efficiency," which was used in Chapter 15 to mean cost per unit. Another term, "outcomes," has become more common as a way of discussing effectiveness. For example, the effectiveness of a police department might be measured by the crime rate. The crime rate is considered to be an outcome or "effect" of police services. The lower the crime rate, the more effective the police force.

Our alternative is to use the phrase "quality of life indicators for the community." While this phrase is longer, more complex and in some ways more jargon-like than the words "effectiveness" and "outcome," we chose it for public discussion for two very important reasons. First, "effectiveness" sounds like and gets confused with the word "efficiency." "Outcome" is clearer but is not part of most people's vocabulary. Second, the term "outcome" implies that the government service is a primary factor in determining the societal condition when it is only one of many factors to consider in the community problem-solving process.

General Population Surveys

How people perceive their community is critical to the survival of elected officials and should be closely monitored through general population surveys. We must distinguish this type of survey from customer surveys. Customer surveys focus on individuals who have recently received a government service and ask them to assess its quality. General population surveys, on the other hand, ask all members of a community for their reflections on a variety of societal conditions. The following case study addresses the societal condition of safety.

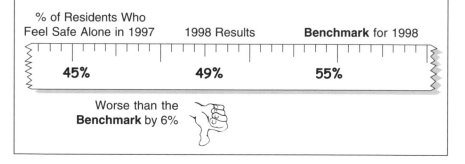

Case Study: Benchmarking the Feeling of Safety in City X

This case study shows how quality of life data can be used to determine the feeling of safety in a community. A basic question that measures safety is whether citizens feel safe when walking alone in their neighborhoods at night. An appropriate benchmark for City X is a 10 percent increase each year in the number of people who feel "safe" or "very safe."

Remember that if you wanted to see the longer trend, you could develop a trend-line graph that shows the trend for the past five, 10 or 20 years. You should also keep in mind that if the city's residents are starting to feel safer, this might be part of a larger national trend. It would help to find governments of comparative size that have been conducting similar research so you can compare your results with those of other communities.

% of Residents Who
Feel Safe Alone in 1997   1998 Results   **Benchmark** for 1998

45%   **49%**   **55%**

Worse than the
Benchmark by 6%

Appendix A provides a step-by-step guide and a generic general population survey form that you can copy and adapt any way you want. You will find that if you do the preparation, create a draft and form a guideline for collecting the responses, you will be ready to conduct the survey. However, such a survey can be costly and should only be undertaken if you have sufficient monetary and personnel resources.

Government Records

At the quality of life level, you're going to be concerned with the big picture. For example, if you're looking at economic development in a state, you look at the state's unemployment rate. If you're concerned about the health conditions in a county, you look at morbidity and mortality rates. The following case study shows the use of government records to determine a benchmark for crime in a city.

Case Study: Comparison of Several Cities to Benchmark Crime

The City X Police Department's fundamental goal is to reduce crime. The most basic unit of crime analysis is Crime Rate per 100,000 Population. An adequate benchmark is to be below the mean of several selected, comparative cities.

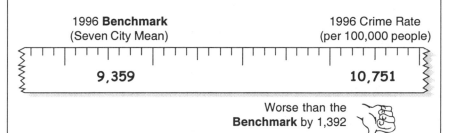

1996 **Benchmark** (Seven City Mean)	1996 Crime Rate (per 100,000 people)
9,359	10,751

Worse than the **Benchmark** by 1,392

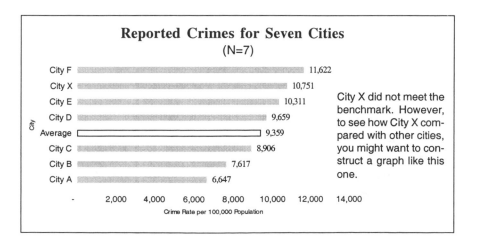

Reported Crimes for Seven Cities
(N=7)

City	Crime Rate per 100,000 Population
City F	11,622
City X	10,751
City E	10,311
City D	9,659
Average	9,359
City C	8,906
City B	7,617
City A	6,647

City X did not meet the benchmark. However, to see how City X compared with other cities, you might want to construct a graph like this one.

2,000   4,000   6,000   8,000   10,000   12,000   14,000

Crime Rate per 100,000 Population

Direct Observation

Another method to examine the "big picture" is direct observation. Direct observation requires training individuals to observe conditions such as street litter and fill out forms correctly. Checks on the way observers complete the form are conducted on a systematic basis. This procedure is costly and can also be applied to study the quality of government services as discussed in Chapter 16. Consult our Web site (www.maxwell.syr.edu/benchmarks) for a direct observation process developed by the Community Benchmarks Program.

Case Study: Using Direct Observation to Determine a Benchmark

A direct observation study of City X in 1998 had the purpose of assessing the physical conditions of observed areas in the six residential subdivisions of the city. The observers looked at the condition of the sidewalks, yards, buildings and parking lots. An observation instrument was designed. Trained undergraduate students performed the observations.

It shows the overall physical condition for each residential sector in City X. For each sector, a random selection of streets was observed on foot by a team of two observers. The study used a scale of 1 to 4, with 1 being the worst and 4 being the best. If you represented Sector 3, you would want your sector to be at or above the six-sector average.

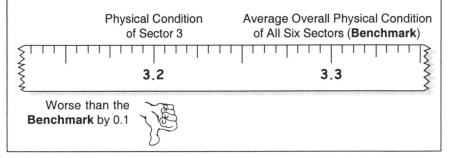

Physical Condition of Sector 3 — 3.2

Average Overall Physical Condition of All Six Sectors (**Benchmark**) — 3.3

Worse than the **Benchmark** by 0.1

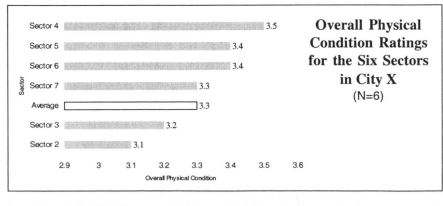

Overall Physical Condition Ratings for the Six Sectors in City X (N=6)

Sector	Overall Physical Condition
Sector 4	3.5
Sector 5	3.4
Sector 6	3.4
Sector 7	3.3
Average	3.3
Sector 3	3.2
Sector 2	3.1

Three Warnings

Warning #1: Do not allow quality of life studies to be too broad and consume too many resources.

The types of benchmarking discussed in this chapter are different from those in previous chapters because the target is not specific to government services but includes the entire community. These benchmarks should be used carefully and in a limited way to highlight both excellent conditions and big problems. Decisions made with long-range consequences such as planning and budgeting are informed by the benchmarks. Because it has such a broad purpose, benchmarking for quality of life improvements in the community can easily gobble up huge resources in time and money with little or no payoff. Some advocates might justify it as having an educational purpose or in changing the culture, but as an elected official, such vague payoffs are not sufficient. Benchmarking to improve a community's quality of life can only be justified if the results clearly feed into planning and budgetary decisions.

Quality of life studies are best performed when designed by a group of community leaders from both within and outside of government. Leaders from not-for-profit organizations, neighborhood groups and business can help bring relevance and acceptance to the studies.

Avoid supporting a quality of life benchmark that everyone agrees is good, but is also out of reach. For example, in an ideal world you would like to see a crime rate of zero. But this is not a realistic benchmark. Instead, consider the more practical benchmark of decreasing the crime rate by 5 percent over the next year.

Warning #2: Do not imply that the government holds primary responsibility for the quality of life in the community.

Given the broad nature of benchmarking, do not make the mistake of holding the government responsible for the benchmark. As we have already indicated, quality of life questions, such as the achievement level of students in the school system or the level of crime, are a result of actions of the entire community. Therefore it is better that you suggest a particular benchmark (such as no increase in the number of vacant houses) as a task for community problem-solving rather than as a job for government action. The government will usually be a key player but will not be the only player. Businesspeople, potential workers, school administrators and those who control economic development funds both within and outside the community are also players. As an elected official, you will want to help lead the community to solve problems, not raise false hope that the government can do it alone.

Warning #3: Do not use benchmarks that are counterproductive.

In choosing quality of life benchmarks for your community, be sure that benchmarks do not drive agencies in the wrong direction. Like all tools, benchmarking can create counterproductive pressures. A classic example of this is the use of the number of arrests, such as speeding, DWI or criminal activity, as the indicator for a benchmark. As noted, setting a high benchmark for the number of arrests ignores the role of other policies, such as prevention. This could lead to decisions to spend money on less effective policies, while addressing prevention could reduce the need to make the arrests in the first place. As an elected official, you must choose your benchmarks carefully to avoid creating more problems.

Benchmarking Quality of Life Measures for Other Government Services

To get an idea of other quality of life measures, look at the list below. Note some measures use general population surveys, while others depend on government records and direct observation.

Examples of Quality of Life Measures for Government Services

Function	"Quality of Life" Indicator
Police	Number of violent crimes per 1,000 population
Fire, Rescue & Emergency Services	Number of structural fires per 1,000 residents
Parks & Recreation	Percent of youth population enrolled in at least one recreation program per year
Transportation	Percent of citizens who rate overall street maintenance quality as "good" or "very good"
Trash Collection & Disposal	Percent of streets found to be free from litter through direct observation
Water Supply	Percent of citizens who rate water services as "good" or "very good"
Building	Percent of housing rated by physical observation as "good" or "very good"
Housing & Community Development	Number of homeless per 1,000 population
Planning	Percent of citizens responding that their proximity to a bus line or stop is "good" or "very good"

Steps for Benchmarking the Quality of Life in a Community

Step 1: Decide if undertaking a quality of life study makes sense in your community. Keep in mind that measuring the efficiency and quality of government services should provide enough information to make informed decisions.

Step 2: Decide which method of quality of life analysis you want to undertake. Both general population surveys and direct observations require a lot of time and resources. Government records will be easier to obtain, but may be dated and difficult to use in comparing municipalities.

Step 3: Before undertaking a general population survey or direct observations, identify all available government records that will be helpful. The more records you identify, the less data you have to collect through surveys and/or direct observations.

Step 4: For the general population survey, there are six steps.

- Become familiar with an existing quality of life study. Several we recommend are *Oregon Benchmarks*, the *City of Portland Service Efforts and Accomplishments* and the *Florida Benchmarks Report*. It's easier to modify an existing study than to create a new one. (See Appendix B for helpful Web sites.)
- Develop the survey using the information provided in Appendix A.
- Test the survey. This will identify any problems with the questions before you send the survey out to the general public.
- Decide how you will distribute the survey.
- Distribute the survey.
- Analyze the results and create the appropriate benchmark tables.

Step 5: For the direct observation method, there are six steps.

- Find any available direct observation studies to use as a model. You can consult our Web site for a sample instrument we have developed.
- Develop the direct observation form.
- Train the researchers who will conduct the direct observation.
- Test the direct observation form and make any necessary changes to it.
- Conduct the direct observations.
- Analyze the results and create the appropriate benchmark tables.

Main Points

✓ Quality of life surveys can be critical in helping you mobilize citizens to work together to solve community problems.

✓ General population surveys can clue you into citizens' perceptions of conditions in your community, but are costly and subject to varied interpretations.

✓ Some government records can be used to assess quality of life, but they are limited because they are frequently outdated and subject to differing opinions.

✓ Direct observation is costly, but can play an important role, especially in assessing the physical environment.

Chapter 18

Gaining Support for Benchmarking

Learn About

✓ How to get your community started on benchmarking

✓ How to advocate for benchmarking

✓ Where to find resources to do benchmarking studies

Implementing meaningful benchmarking studies does not mean your efforts will improve local government performance. The world is full of reports based on solid research presented through beautiful charts and graphs that have had no impact, or, even worse, a negative impact. If you are an elected official, you probably already have some good ideas on how to get your colleagues and the community to use benchmarks effectively. This chapter is directed to elected government officials because the philosophy of continuous improvement implicit in the idea of benchmarking needs to be embraced by those in power. Citizens and those challenging the incumbents can also use the advice in this chapter as they seek to promote benchmarking.

Getting Started

As an elected government official, you have a platform from which to stimulate the use of benchmarks. However, the degree to which you push benchmarking depends on your official position and your relationships with other officials and powerful groups. If you are the chief executive of your town, you can probably make more headway in getting your departments to use benchmarking than if you are a first-time elected council member.

The best place to start is with yourself. Benchmarking and the attitude of continuous improvement should become an ingrained part of your politics and decision-making. When you make proposals, give your hoped-for results in very specific terms, such as "reduce telephone costs by 10 percent" or "investigate complaints about code violations within 24 hours." Almost as important as the first step in developing a benchmarking mind-set is to call for point-of-service customer surveys in government offices that work with the public. When you enter the treacherous arena of community problem-solving, you could challenge everyone to reduce the amount of litter in public parks so that hours spent by public works on litter removal is 50 percent less.

You should see benchmarking as both a process to be encouraged throughout your government and an educational effort with long-term consequences. If you can get others to think in terms of collecting systematic information on indicators and then setting goals for the government and the community, you will raise the level of discussions in your community and improve government performance. This is the reason that we suggested that our minimum goal is to get you to ask the right questions, even if you do not use the formal term "benchmarking."

Inviting other government officials and citizens to join you in deciding what goals to use as the basis for your benchmarking is a sensible way to begin. Here are three reasons:

- Promotes the benchmarking mind-set
- Structures discussions so people can communicate more clearly
- Ensures you will be benchmarking what key stakeholders think is important

Discussions of what goals should be benchmarked moves players and citizens beyond vague conversations. Instead of making general statements about how trash collection services should cost less or park programs should be improved, for example, discussions involving benchmarking should encourage specific targets so everyone can be on the same page. This can be done through informal conversations in which you pose a question to a department head by asking for a specific target, or to a group in a neighborhood that would like to see a cleaner local park.

You can also use more formal procedures. If you are giving a talk at a local community organization that is concerned about teenagers who loiter on the corner, you could suggest that the organization state specifically how long and where it is acceptable for teenagers to hang out. If the staff of the assessor's office is concerned about customer satisfaction, you could ask the group to come up with a specific way to measure customer satisfaction, and to set a goal for that measure.

The most formal process used to determine benchmarks is conducting structured focus group meetings. A focus group is a set of individuals who react to questions or cues through informal discussion. The goal is to have one or more focus group meetings, with five to 12 people, who express their ideas about a particular topic.

Case Study: Using High School Focus Groups to Come Up With Benchmarks

The Maxwell Community Benchmarks Program helped students organize a set of focus groups at a local suburban high school. More than 300 students, teachers, parents, school board officials and administrators met in 28 different focus groups conducted by members of the high school's senior class.

The basic question asked was: What goals should the entire high school program achieve? More than 100 goals were developed, but a consensus emerged around several that included: students should have a working knowledge of personal finance, should vote in local elections and should succeed in college. These and a few other general goals received support across all 28 meetings. The students came up with ways of measuring each goal that included tests, surveys, reviewing voting records and interviewing alumni of the school who had graduated three years earlier and gone to college.

The focus group served to build legitimacy and consensus for the benchmarks that were developed. The entire process became part of the high school's planning and decision-making.

Advocating Benchmarking

The benefits that have been described allow you to make a strong case for benchmarking. How you present that position depends upon your personal style. You may want to take a low-key approach by using public opportunities to ask citizens and colleagues to identify important goals and indicators to measure those goals. Or you may want to take a more assertive position by being a strong advocate for improving government through benchmarking. If so, two model speeches follow that you can adapt and use. Incumbents and challengers can use these speeches.

Model Speeches

Advocating the Benchmarking of Government Services

I am strongly committed to providing the best government service for the lowest possible cost. Fortunately, we can learn a great deal from the most successful businesses in the United States. They are successful because they work to continuously improve their products and services.

One of the ways they do this is by keeping good records on the resources they use and the results of their efforts. They set goals to improve their products and services so they have more satisfied consumers, while they control costs by establishing benchmarks of high quality and efficient production.

We can do the same thing for all the services our government provides our citizens. We can monitor and compare our costs, our workload, the quality of our services and conditions in the community, and we can set goals to strive for. We can have benchmarks to continuously improve our government services. I am proposing a plan to get all of our departments to use the tool of benchmarking, which has returned American business to first place in the world.

Benchmarks for Quality of Life

We live in a great community that has been getting better each year. Our (list of those things everyone would agree is good about the town) are outstanding. However difficult challenges lie ahead for all of us. We must pull together so we can do our best to protect and enhance the quality of life we now enjoy.

To help us succeed, I strongly urge we use benchmarking techniques, which have proved to be very helpful throughout many areas of the United States. A benchmark is an indicator that tells us about some aspect of society, such as acreage of parks or the level of crime, and sets a goal for where we would like to be.

The technique has been used in business to improve profits and in government to improve the community. We can use it in the same way – to bring us all together to meet the challenges our community will face in the next decade and beyond.

Another way of advocating the use of benchmarks is to create or participate in scorecarding exercises. Scorecarding is increasingly popular in newspapers, magazine and books where municipalities are ranked for such things as quality of life, clean environment and good schools. An example appears below.

Tip for Advanced Users: Scorecarding

Metropolitan Area Suburb Rankings for Crime

Municipality	Rank
Berkely Heights, NJ	1
Ridgewood, NJ	2
Stony Point, NY	3
New Providence, NJ	4
Wycoff, NJ	5
Tenafly, NJ	6
Glen Rock, NJ	7
Oakland, NJ	8
Ringwood, NJ	9
Hanover Township, NJ	10

Scorecarding allows you to display the information you have collected into an easy-to-read format. The data on the left is taken from the *American Suburbs Rating Guide and Fact Book (1993)*, which rates 1,770 suburbs surrounding 50 major metropolitan areas.

The chart displays rankings for crime for the New York, Northern New Jersey and Long Island metropolitan area suburbs, with one (Berkely Heights) being the best. *The Guide* used the violent crime rate and the property crime rate to create the rankings.

As you can see, scorecarding is most useful when comparing municipalities. The results are displayed in an easy-to-read format. Communities can set a target for their collective efforts – to be in the top 10. Politicians, businesses, citizens groups, the police department and a whole range of not-for-profit and government organizations in a town that did not appear in the top ten would be well advised to view these top 10 communities as the benchmark and take action to close the gap.

Scorecarding usually gets a lot of attention, but it can have a negative effect. Even if your town scores high (like Stoney Point in the example), citizens can complain about not being #1.

Finding Resources for Benchmarking Statistics

The amount of work depends on what you are benchmarking and whether you use the analysis over time or comparative analysis approach. In general, data on costs, workload and efficiency are less expensive to collect than information on the quality of government services and on the quality of life. Analysis over time comparisons for one unit are much less costly than comparisons across several units. The figure below lists the costs of benchmarking studies from most expensive to least expensive.

Benchmarking Studies Ranked From Most Expensive to Least Expensive

Type of Analysis	Benchmark Goals
Comparative Analysis	Quality of LIfe
Analysis Over Time	Quality of Government Services Workload of Government Services
Absolute	Cost of Government Services

As a single elected official, it is unlikely that you will embark on a benchmarking study of your own for anything more than an analysis over time of costs or workloads. You need help to do more. You can search for this help in the following places:

♦ Your municipality provides the resources by allocating staff, providing funds for additional staff or by hiring an outside consultant.

♦ Your municipality joins others to collect comparative data, which requires each municipality to allocate either staff or funds.

♦ You receive funds from business or not-for-profit organizations in the community to hire an outside consultant, or they volunteer staff to provide the necessary professional support.

♦ You contact educational institutions to support your effort either through an internship or a class project. In some rare cases, a high school class might be able to help.

Here are some comments on some of these alternatives. First, beware of the outside consultant route. Outside consultants tend not to believe that less is more. You may end up paying a lot for a study that has limited utility. In addition, since outside consultants are professional researchers, they may use too much jargon. You must be prepared and highly sophisticated to work with an outside consultant. It is a path you might take after a few preliminary endeavors conducted by you or existing staff members. Finally, to be effective over the long run, benchmarking must be incorporated into the procedures of your government. Using an outside consultant may lead to the view that benchmarking is something out of the ordinary. Outside consultants can be a viable route only if you find the right consultant, have very specific objectives in mind and have a plan to incorporate some of the work into the daily operations of your government.

A less costly and highly effective alternative would be to use high school or college undergraduate and graduate students. Some teachers and professors have students undertake real world social science projects. If you can find one, you can have them collect and analyze data using the guidelines provided throughout this manual. For example, in one community the mayor had a high school class complete a study of parking problems and the police department used the information to reduce illegal parking.

At Syracuse University's Maxwell School, both undergraduate and graduate programs often complete applied research projects. The Master of Public Administration Program requires students to take a three-week workshop where small teams work for outside clients. One such team designed and field tested the direct observation study discussed earlier. At the undergraduate level, policy studies students complete studies for local government and not-for-profit agencies. Students in this program have completed several customer survey studies. Research, valued at more than $100,000 a year by the clients served, has been completed. More information on these programs is on our Web site at www.maxwell.syr.edu/benchmarks.

The Maxwell programs are considered by most outside observers as best practices in the education of citizens and future government officials. Many schools have similar programs at the graduate level. For example, the Kennedy School at Harvard provides a program similar to the MPA workshop program. Schools of public affairs, which are members of the National Association of Schools of Public Affairs and Administration (NASPAA), are at www.NASPAA.org/programs/index.html. If you live within 100 miles of one of those schools, you might want to contact them. Unfortunately, few undergraduate programs provide similar services.

As a government official, you are likely to get a warm reception if you approach your local university, college, or high school. However, this does not mean you will get a definite commitment to do your research. Your best chance would be if such a program already exists. However, if none exists, we suggest two strategies.

- ◆ Try to get an intern. Call the institution's "intern office." If there is no central office, ask the chancellor's or president's office which departments have internships. A single intern who gives you 45 hours per credit earned (which happens usually in chunks of 3 credits or 135 hours of work) could provide a benchmarking study.
- ◆ Find a professor who either already does or would be interested in incorporating such a study in class. You could ask around. If you have difficulty, the best strategy would be to write a formal letter on government stationery to the chancellor or president, with a copy to the institution's government affairs office, if one exists.

A sample letter appears below.

Sample Letter: Requesting Help for Benchmarking

As an elected government official, I strive to improve our community in many ways. I know that _____[name of the college] is a first-class resource for research and is also deeply committed to serving our community. For this reason, I am asking that you provide me with assistance in a project to improve local government services and the quality of life in our community.

Could you please arrange for me to contact a member of your faculty who might be willing to take on a class project or to supervise an intern to complete a study that would provide information to benchmark _____[name the service area]? I would need the study to be undertaken during the _____ semester and to involve about ____ hours of student work. Students would have the opportunity to present their findings at appropriate venues, including the town board.

Thank you very much for your time. I would appreciate hearing from you no later than _____ [give the respondent about two weeks] on whether there is someone with whom I can discuss this project's feasibility.

Sincerely,

[your name]

Main Points

✓ Get yourself in a mind-set to benchmark.

✓ Try to encourage colleagues and other groups to list benchmarks in informal meetings and focus groups.

✓ Advocate for benchmarking as part of your political platform.

✓ Think about starting or supporting a scorecarding study if you think major improvements are needed.

✓ Recognize the resources needed to conduct benchmarking studies and seek them from a variety of sources.

Supplemental Information

Easy Guide for Customer and General Population Surveys

Surveys provide valuable information to local officials and community members. Done properly, surveys can indicate how citizens rate local services and how the general public perceives the quality of life in a community.

There is, however, considerable public skepticism about surveys. Critics often question the way questions are written and who was surveyed. For local officials and the public to accept results, follow four basic rules:

- ◆ Be clear about whether the focus is on the experiences of specific customers of services (customer surveys), or on the general perceptions of community members (quality of life surveys).
- ◆ Write surveys in clear language and test before distribution.
- ◆ Develop a specific, practical plan for distributing surveys to customers of services or for contacting community members.
- ◆ Present results so they are easily understood.

If these are not considered, you may find yourself at a meeting of local officials or at a public meeting with skeptics dismissing what you have done and you will wonder if your work was to no avail.

Customer and Quality of Life Surveys

Chapter 16 discusses customer surveys and Chapter 17 discusses quality of life surveys. The first step in conducting a survey is to be clear about whether you wish to know about the experiences of those who have actually used a local service, or whether you wish to know about the perceptions of all members of the community.

If the goal is to determine the views of people using services, the survey should focus on identifiable customers. Even if the concern is something general, such as the condition of roads, the relevant population is those who drive and use the roads.

Dr. Jeffrey Stonecash, professor of political science at the Maxwell School at Syracuse University, prepared the initial draft of this appendix.

If the quality of life focus is chosen, the results will include members of the community who have vague impressions of the community but perhaps no actual experience with some services. Many residents of a community, for example, will not know how well property assessment is handled because they probably have never questioned their own assessment. They may not frequent community parks. If all residents are surveyed, many will respond on the basis of their general perceptions of the community and not on the basis of experience. Therefore, general population surveys are best used when asking such quality of life questions as, "how safe do you feel" and "do you think there are enough public parks?"

Writing and Testing Surveys

In writing surveys, your goals should be to:

- *Create a survey that is short enough that people will be willing to answer it, but asks questions about matters important to you.* Regardless of whether the survey is of customers or the general community, most people do not want to answer more than one page of questions.

- For *customer surveys* it is particularly important to have a one-page survey. Many of these surveys will be distributed to those who come to a particular office for some service and wish to leave as quickly as possible. If surveys are mailed to customers, or calls are made to them, it is generally possible to ask people to complete a two-page survey, but a one-page survey is preferable.

- For *quality of life surveys* distributed in the mail or presented to residents via telephone calls, limit the survey to one or two pages to ensure higher completion rates.

- *Write questions that present people with clear and specific alternatives as answers.* This makes it easy for those completing the survey to know what kinds of responses you are seeking. Use categories such as "yes or no," "satisfactory or unsatisfactory," "very good, good, fair, or poor." Using these categories will also make it easy for you to record and tally the results. You may wish to include an open-ended question that asks for general comments. While these answers are often valuable, they are difficult to record with any uniformity.

- *Use the same alternatives as response choices so you can compare responses for different questions.* This allows you to compare aspects of service or different aspects of community life to see areas that need improvement. For example, in asking about the quality of services, you may wish to ask about the clarity of printed documents, speed of responding to a request and courteousness of the staff. If the responses for every service are "very good, good, fair and poor," it makes comparison much easier. If different alternatives are used, comparison across questions becomes very difficult. The same principle applies to quality of life surveys. If you wish to compare sense of public safety, cleanliness of parks and maintenance of roads, it will be valuable to see which receive high ratings.

◆ *Avoid "biasing" the responses.* Do not ask questions that exclude positive or negative answers. Questions should not be phrased in a way that makes an alternate answer appear to be incorrect. If the question is biased, the results will be suspect.

  ▾ *Example of bias*: If you ask the question: "Wouldn't you agree that most services in this town are generally good?" most people will probably agree for two reasons, both of which involve bias. First, the question focuses on most services and few people are likely to find "most" services deficient. Second, the word "wouldn't" pushes people to agree. Because few people are likely to say that they disagree, the findings that are produced will be inaccurate.

  ▾ *Example of no bias*: Please rate trash collection services in this community on a scale of 1-5 with one being very poor and five being very good. A six means you have no opinion. This question is specific (trash collection services vs. most services), the range of choices is broad and the question is phrased in a neutral way.

◆ *Conduct a pilot test of the survey before distribution.* Ask the questions of at least five people who will tell you if:

  ▾ the directions are clear
  ▾ they understand the questions and the possible responses
  ▾ the survey is easy to read
  ▾ the choices seem fair
  ▾ the right topics are addressed

Based on their feedback, make the changes and then ask your reviewers to read the survey once more.

Note for Web Users

The surveys on the following pages, along with others, can downloaded in Microsoft Word™ the Community Benchmarks Program Web site at www.maxwell.syr.edu/benchmarks.

Model Surveys

Two sample surveys follow. The first is a customer survey that you can distribute to those people who come to an office. The second is a quality of life survey that you can mail to residents or present through a telephone call. Each survey is short and uses the same set of responses throughout. This makes it easy for the respondent to complete the survey and for you to tally the results.

Model Customer Survey

Customer Survey for Office of: [your office name]

1. What service did you request?

2. Please rate this service in the following areas:

	Poor	Fair	Good	Very Good	N/A
a. Speed of staff in responding to you	1	2	3	4	5
b. Helpfulness and friendliness of staff	1	2	3	4	5
c. Staff knowledge of service you requested	1	2	3	4	5
d. Overall treatment by staff	1	2	3	4	5
e. Clarity of written materials presented to you (if any)	1	2	3	4	5
f. Clarity of guidelines on relevant forms (if any)	1	2	3	4	5
g. Satisfaction with how your specific service request was handled	1	2	3	4	5
h. Overall quality of service received	1	2	3	4	5

3. What suggestions would you make to improve service in this office?

Thank you for your responses. If you would like us to contact you, please provide your name and telephone number:

Name: Telephone Number:

Model Quality of Life Survey

The [town/village/city] of [name of town] is conducting a survey of community residents about your perceptions of the quality of life here. (If mail survey) Could you please take a few minutes to fill out the survey below and mail it back to us in the envelope provided? (If telephone survey) Could I have just two minutes of your time to ask you a few questions?

All responses are confidential.

1. Overall, how would you rate the quality of life in this community:

❑ Poor   ❑ Fair   ❑ Good   ❑ Very Good   ❑ No Opinion

2. How would you rate the following aspects of life in this community (poor, fair, good, or very good)?

Specific Aspect Of Community	Evaluation Responses				
	Poor	Fair	Good	Very Good	N/A
a. Safety from crime.	1	2	3	4	5
b. Traffic – ability to get around.	1	2	3	4	5
c. Quality of road surfaces.	1	2	3	4	5
d. Facilities in parks (courts, fields, play areas).	1	2	3	4	5
e. Schools.	1	2	3	4	5
f. Availability of good jobs.	1	2	3	4	5
g. Garbage pickup.	1	2	3	4	5
h. Availability of reasonably priced housing.	1	2	3	4	5
i. Government response to problems.	1	2	3	4	5
j. Quality of libraries.	1	2	3	4	5

3. What suggestions would you make to improve the quality of life in this community?

4. What do you see as the major problem facing this community?

5. Age: 6. Sex: ❑ Male   ❑ Female

7. Area of the community you live in:

Thank you for your responses.

Soliciting Responses to Customer Surveys

Decide Whom You Wish to Survey

Do you want to survey people who come into an office to request assistance or to file a complaint? Or do you want to survey people who have contacted a government office by mail or phone?

Surveying Customers at an Office

You probably cannot survey all users because you don't have the staff to record all of the responses. Develop a systematic plan to solicit responses from some subset of all users. Try to obtain a random sample by asking every third, fifth or 10th user, depending on the volume of users, to fill out a survey. That helps minimize the problem of only satisfied or dissatisfied users responding. To help you keep track of the number of users, you could keep a clipboard at the desk in each office and ask every customer to sign in before you deal with them. That will make counting easier. Using such a list will also make it easier to manage customers when they come in bunches, such as lunchtime or during tax assessment season. Customers will probably also appreciate the sense of orderliness with which you respond to them, and they will experience less anxiety about having to jockey for position. If you decide to mail to customers, then be sure to also have them include their address so that you will have a complete mailing list.

Surveying Customers Calling in to an Office

A log of callers would also make it possible to send every 10th or 20th person a survey and ask them to return it. These surveys should be sent with a self-addressed envelope with postage paid by the local government. This will result in a higher response rate.

Surveying Customers Using a Government Facility

If the purpose is to gather assessments from users of a facility such as parks or libraries, there should be a plan to visit parks and ask people using them to fill out surveys. Remember that different groups use parks at different times. Walkers, runners and tennis players may visit in the early morning. Parents with children may visit in the late morning and early afternoon. Teenagers may spend more time at the park in the evenings. Others may come to parks only on weekends. Make sure to solicit responses across different times and days to include various types of customers. Again, do not ask every visitor, but develop a plan of asking every fifth (or whatever) person, depending on the number of users.

Soliciting Responses to Quality of Life Surveys

Bias in Responses

When presenting results to either the public or your own staff, the major source of skepticism, aside from how questions were asked, will be doubts about who filled out the surveys. If the results are positive, critics will ask if you got your supporters to complete the surveys. If they are critical, the staff will wonder if all the cranks and complainers in the community filled them out. The most difficult situation you will face is to be in a meeting and have someone loudly ask, "Who filled these out? None of my friends ever were asked to," and to have no answer about your steps to make sure everyone had a chance to fill out the surveys. The critics will be arguing about bias. They suspect some people were intentionally or unintentionally included or excluded and that the results are a product of who was included. Your goal in acquiring responses should be to make sure that everyone who is relevant to the survey has a chance to participate.

The crucial matter for the credibility of a survey to its users is not how many people were surveyed, but whether those who participated roughly reflect the relevant group in the community.

To avoid the criticism of shaping the results, develop a practical plan that gives everyone a chance to participate, or makes the process random. If you develop such a plan and can explain it to critics, you may not quiet them, but you may convince other customers that you tried to avoid the bias problem in your reports.

Decide Whether to Call or Mail

Decide whether you have the capability to call community members or should mail surveys. Telephone surveys have the advantage of being relatively quick to conduct, and you can get a good number of responses by this route. You also do not have to pay postage. The difficulty is that you need many phones and staff members willing to call at night. Most people will be at home in the evening, which is the best time to call. If you don't have both of these, you can mail surveys, as long as you can afford the printing costs, the postage and staff time.

Select a List

Develop a plan that makes sure all members of the community have a chance to participate. Think about how each list of community members might exclude some members and choose the list (which may not be perfect) that will exclude the fewest community members. Here are some examples of lists that might be used and the problems of each.

- ◆ *Voter registration lists*: These lists involve voters, about whom elected officials care, and generally contain telephone numbers and addresses, making access possible. The limitation is that many people, especially younger citizens and those with lower incomes do not register to vote. Someone who knows that may argue that this list does not represent the whole community.

- ◆ *Local property taxpayer lists*: These lists generally have very complete information, so you can call or mail everyone. Renters, however, do not pay local property taxes, so you can be accused of excluding them.

- ◆ *Telephone lists*: These lists have telephone numbers and most have addresses. Since almost everyone has a telephone number, this will include both renters and those not registered, so it may be your best list. It also primarily includes adults, who are the focus of most community surveys. The primary limitation is that those with unlisted numbers will not be on the list. Unless there is information indicating that those with unlisted numbers tend to be a particular type (older, for example), you are safest with this list.

Develop a Plan to Contact a Limited, but Random, Number of People

You cannot call or mail everyone in a community. Decide how many completed surveys you want (say 300), and then assume that some people on the list you start with will have moved, some will refuse and some will not be there when you call. Assume that if you call a list over several nights or mail to a list, you will get responses from about 20 percent. That means you must start with a list of about 1,500 people to end up with 300 responses (1,500/.20=300).

Next you need to determine the total number of people on your list. If you start with an original list of 15,000 names, divide that by 1,500 (15,000/1,500=100). This means you want to survey every 100th person on the list to ensure a random sample, meaning you did not intentionally include or exclude any particular community member. Start at the beginning of your list. Survey the first person, skip 100, survey the next person, skip 100 and so forth. If the list is a telephone book, call or mail to every hundreth person. If the initial number is 7,500, call or mail to every fifth person.

Include Demographic Questions to Allow Comparison with the Entire Community

Include a few questions on demographics (sex, age, area) to make it possible to indicate how your group of respondents compares with the general community. By questioning respondents on where they live you will be able to make a statement like the following: Forty percent of all residents live in the northern area of the community; 38 percent of respondents are from that area. Statements like these will be valuable when critics question whom you called because they demonstrate a representative sample of the general community.

Presenting Information

Explain the Process

To reassure readers that the process of gathering information was done in a reasonable and fair way, write a one-page summary of how you distributed surveys. This will ward off critics who are skeptical of the process and results. Put the explanation at the end of your report, along with the survey, but indicate at the beginning that the explanation is provided at the back. Always include a copy of the complete survey.

Use Complete, Clear and Simple Presentations

When you present results, include the full question and the alternatives given to respondents. The total number of responses, the number choosing each response and the percentage in each category should be presented. The example below provides a suggestion about how to make the results clear to readers. Be sure the information is easy to read and absorb.

Sample Presentation of Results

Q: Rate the Overall Quality of Life in the Community
(Entire community; responses sum down to 100 percent)

Responses	Number	Percent
Poor	200	13
Fair	200	13
Good	400	27
Very good	600	40
No opinion	100	7
Total # Responding	**1,500**	**100**

Present Results by Categories

It is often valuable to present results by groups and areas of a community to assess whether satisfaction with services varies by group or neighborhood within a community. This allows the development of a strategy to respond to groups or areas where higher levels of dissatisfaction exist.

In making such presentations, use the same format for presenting results so readers can easily view and interpret the results. The example below presents the percentages who choose different responses for the entire community, and then for different areas of the community. If presented this way, it is possible to see that satisfaction with the general quality of life is much lower in the north than it is in the south or elsewhere.

Sample Presentation of Results

Q: Rate the Overall Quality of Life in the Community
(Responses sum down to 100 percent)

Responses	Entire Community		Area of Community		
	Number	Percent	North	South	All Other
Poor	200	13	25	7	7
Fair	200	13	24	9	9
Good	400	27	32	18	21
Very good	600	40	11	60	57
No opinion	100	7	8	7	7
Total	**1,500**	**100**	**100**	**100**	**100**

Helpful Web Sites, Organizations and Publications

The purpose of this section is to provide you with additional tools to help you to develop your own checklist and benchmarks. A variety of Web sites and organizations are described as well as some key publications. The danger of being inundated with too much information is real. You should be selective and use this index as a starting point.

Web Sites and Organizations

Contact information is provided for each organization.

The authors and the Community Benchmarks Program of the Syracuse University Maxwell School of Citizenship and Public Affairs maintain a Web site at www.maxwell.syr.edu/benchmarks, which offers supplemental information and links to relevant Web sites. The Web page will be periodically updated.

**Academy for State
& Local Government**
444 North Capitol Street, NW
Suite 345
Washington, DC 20001
Tel. 202 434-4850
Fax 202 434-4851
www.althing.com/pia

American Planning Association
122 South Michigan Avenue,
Suite 1600
Chicago, IL 60603
Tel. 312 431-9100
Fax 312 431-9985
www.planning.org

American Public Health Association
1015 15th Street, NW, 3rd Floor
Washington, DC 20005
Tel. 202 789-5600
Fax 202 789-5661
www.apha.org

**American Public Human
Services Association**
810 1st Street, NE, Suite 500
Washington, DC 20002
Tel. 202 682-0100
Fax 202 289-6555
www.aphsa.org

**American Public
Power Association**
2301 M Street, NW, 3rd Floor
Washington, DC 20037
Tel. 202 467-2900
Fax 202 467-2910
www.appanet.org

**American Public Transit
Association**
1201 New York Avenue, NW
Washington, DC 2005
Tel. 202 898-4000
Fax 202 898-4049
www.apta.com

American Public Works Association
2345 Grand Boulevard, Suite 500
Kansas City, MO 64108-2625
Tel. 816 472-6100
Fax 816 472-1610
www.apwa.net
Email apwa@apwa.net

American Society for Public Administration
1120 G Street, NW, Suite 700
Washington, DC 20005
Tel. 202 393-7878
Fax 202 638-4952
www.aspanet.org

American Water Works Association
6666 West Quincy Avenue
Denver, CO 80235
Tel. 303 347-6135
Fax 303 795-1440
www.awwa.org

Association for Governmental Leasing & Financing
1200 19th Street, NW, Suite 300
Washington, DC 20036-2422
Tel. 202 429-5135
Fax 202 429-5113
www.aglf.org
Email aglf@dc.sba.com

Association of State & Interstate Water Pollution Control Administrators
750 1st Street, NW, Suite 1010
Washington, DC 20002
Tel. 202 898-0905
Fax 202 898-0929
www.asiwpca.org
Email admin1@clark.net

Building Officials & Code Administrators, International
4051 West Flossmoor Road
Country Club Hills, IL 60478-5795
Tel. 708 799-2300
Fax 708 799-4981
www.bocai.org

Council for Urban Economic Development
1730 K Street, NW, Suite 700
Washington, DC 20006
Tel. 202 223-4735
Fax 202 223-4745
http://cued.org

Government Finance Officers Association
180 North Michigan Avenue, Suite 800
Chicago, IL 60601
Tel. 312 977-9700
Fax 312 977-4806
www.gfoa.org

Institute of Transportation Engineers
525 School Street, NW, Suite 410
Washington, DC 20024-2797
Tel. 202 554-8050
Fax 202 863-5486
www.ite.org

International Association of Assessing Officers
130 East Randolph Street, Suite 850
Chicago, IL 60601
Tel. 312 819-6100
Fax 312 819-6149
www.iaao.org

International Association of Chiefs of Police
515 North Washington Street
Alexandria, VA 22314-2357
Tel. 703 836-6767
Fax 703 836-4543
www.theiacp.org

International Association of Fire Chiefs
4025 Fair Ridge Drive
Fairfax, VA 22033-2868
Tel. 703 273-0911
Fax 703 273-9363
www.iafc.org

**International Association
of Fish & Wildlife**
444 North Capitol Street, NW,
Suite 544
Washington, DC 20001
Tel. 202 624-7890
Fax 202 624-7891
iafwa@sso.org

**International Bridge, Tunnel
& Turnpike Association**
2120 L Street, NW, Suite 305
Washington, DC 20037
Tel. 202 659-4620
Fax 202 659-0500
www.ibtta.org

**International City/County
Management Association**
777 North Capitol Street, NE, 5th Floor
Washington, DC 20002
Tel. 202 962-3604
Fax 202 962-3500
www.icma.org

**International Downtown
Association**
910 17th Street, NW, Suite 210
Washington, DC 20006
Tel. 202 293-4505
Fax 202 293-4509
www.ida-downtown.org
Email question@ida-downtown.org

**International Institute
of Municipal Clerks**
1212 North San Dimas Canyon Road
San Dimas, CA 91773
Tel. 909 592-4462
Fax 909 592-1555
Email iimchq@aol.com

**International Municipal
Lawyers Association**
1110 Vermont Avenue, NW, Suite 200
Washington, DC 20005
Tel. 202 466-5424
Fax 202 785-0152
www.imla.org
Email info@imla.org

**International Personnel
Management Association**
1617 Duke Street
Alexandria, VA 22314
Tel. 703 549-7100
Fax 703 684-0948
www.ipma-hr.org
Email ipma@ipma-hr.org

**National Academy
of Public Administration**
1120 G Street, NW, Suite 850
Washington, DC 20005
Tel. 202 347-3190
Fax 202 393-0993
www.napawash.org

**National Academy of Public
Administration – Alliance for
Redesigning Government**
1120 G Street, NW, Suite 850
Washington, DC 20005
Tel. 202 347-3190
Fax 202 347-3252

National Association of Counties
440 1st Street, NW
Washington, DC 20001
Tel. 202 942-4201
Fax 202 942-4203
www.naco.org

**National Association of
Development Organizations**
444 North Capitol Street, NW,
Suite 630
Washington, DC 20001
Tel. 202 624-7806
Fax 202 624-8813
Email nado@sso.org

**National Association of
Government Communicators**
526 King Street #423
Alexandria, VA 22314
Tel. 703 4369
Fax 703 706-9583
www.nagc.com
Email info@nagc.com

National Association of Housing & Redevelopment Officials
630 Eye Street, NW
Washington, DC 20001-3736
Tel. 202 289-3500
Fax 202 289-8181
www.nahro.org

National Association of Regional Councils
1700 K Street, NW, Suite 1300
Washington, DC 20006
Tel. 202 457-0710
Fax 202 296-9352
http://narc.org/narc

National Association of Telecommunications Officers & Advisors
1650 Tysons Boulevard, Suite 200
McLean, VA 22102
Tel. 703 506-3275
Fax 703 506-3266
www.natoa.org

National Associations of Towns & Townships
444 North Capitol Street, NW,
Suite 208
Washington, DC 20001
Tel. 202 624-3550
Fax 202 624-3554
www.natat.org
Email natat@sso.org

National Civic League
1445 Market Street, Suite 300
Denver, CO 80202-1717
Tel. 303 571-4343
Fax 303 571-4343
www.ncl.org
Email ncl@ncl.org

National Community Development Association
5222 1st Street, NW, Suite 120
Washington, DC 20006
Tel. 202 293-7587
Fax 202 887-5546
www.ncdaonline.org
Email ncda@ncdaonline.org

National Conference of States Building Codes & Standards
505 Huntmar Park Drive, #210
Herndon, VA 20170
Tel. 703 437-0100
Fax 703 481-3596
www.ncsbcs.org

National League of Cities
1301 Pennsylvania Avenue, NW,
Suite 550
Washington, DC 20004
Tel. 202 626-3143
Fax 202 626-3043
www.ncl.org

National Public Employer Labor Relations Association
1620 Eye Street, NW, 4th Floor
Washington, DC 20006
Tel. 202 296-2230
Fax 202 293-2352
www.npelra.org

National Recreation & Park Association
22377 Belmont Ridge Road
Ashburn, VA 20148
Tel. 703 858-0784
Fax 703 858-0794
www.nrpa.org
Email info@nrpa.org

National Society for Professional Engineers
1420 King Street
Alexandria, VA 22314
Tel. 703 694-2800
Fax 703 836-4875
www.nspe.org

Police Executive Research Forum
1120 Connecticut Avenue, NW
Suite 930
Washington, DC 20036
Tel. 202 466-7820
Fax 202 466-7826
www.policeforum.org
Email perf@policeforum.org

Police Foundation
1201 Connecticut Avenue, NW,
Suite 200
Washington, DC 20036
Tel. 202 833-1460
Fax 202 659-9149
www.policefoundation.org
Email pfinfo@policefoundation.org

Public Administration Service
7927 Jones Branch Drive,
Suite 100 South
McLean, VA 22102
Tel. 703 734-8970
Fax 703 734-4965
www.pasq.org
Email postmaster@pasq.org

Public Risk Management Association
1815 North Ft. Myer Drive,

Suite 1020
Arlington, VA 22209
Tel. 703 528-7701
Fax 703 528-7966

Public Technology, Inc.
1301 Pennsylvania Avenue, NW,
Suite 800
Washington, DC 20004
Tel. 202 626-2426
Fax 202 626-2498
http://pti.nw.dc.us
Email press@pti.nw.dc.us

The US Conference of Mayors
1620 Eye Street, NW, 4th Floor
Washington, DC 20006
Tel. 202 293-7330
Fax 202 293-2352
www.usmayors.org

Annotated Bibliography

The books and reports listed here cover only a part of the growing literature on benchmarking for the public sector. We used many of these sources to create this guide.

Ammons, David, ed. *Accountability for Performance: Measurement and Monitoring in Local Government*. Washington, DC: ICMA, 1995.

A collection of articles that covers how to develop performance measures and also how to ensure the system's success.

Ammons, David A. *Municipal Benchmarks: Assessing Performance and Establishing Community Standards*. Thousand Oaks, California: Sage Publications, Inc, 1996.

Provides a basic introduction to benchmarking and also provides a list of indicators for a wide variety of government services. Also provides data for indicators from selected cities.

Comptroller's Special Report on Municipal Affairs: For Local Fiscal Year Ended in 1997. Albany, NY: Office of the State Comptroller, Division of Municipal Affairs, December 1998.

Contains financial information for all counties, towns, villages and school districts in New York state. It is an excellent source for preliminary information on cost analysis. Similar publications should exist for each municipality in other states.

Florida Commission on Government Accountability to the People. *The Florida Benchmarks Report: February 1996.* Tallahassee, Florida: Executive Office of the Governor, 1996.

Similar to the Oregon Benchmarks, this source is also helpful when constructing quality of life studies.

Hatry, Harry P. et al. *How Effective Are Your Community Services? Procedures for Measuring Their Quality.* Washington, DC: The Urban Institute and the ICMA, 1992.

Provides effectiveness measures for a variety of government services. Also provides suggestions for data sources for each indicator.

International City/Council Management Association and the Urban Institute. *Comparative Performance Measurement: FY 1995 Data Report.* Washington, DC: ICMA, 1997.

Provides examples of indicators for many government services. Displays indicator data in graphical format.

Municipal Reference Guide: New York (Northern Edition – 1997-98). Eatontown, NJ: National Resource Directories, Inc., 1997.

Features data for towns and villages in Northern New York. Includes background information on financial, housing and demographic data. The company publishes similar guides for New Jersey, New York, Pennsylvania, Illinois and Virginia. The company's Web site is http://towndata.com.

Office of the City Auditor. *City of Portland Service Efforts and Accomplishments: 1997.* **Portland, Oregon: Office of the City Auditor, 1998.**

A very useful source for any method of benchmarking. This study is an example of what kind of information cities and municipalities should collect to be able to measure the efficiency and quality of their government services. Many of the examples throughout our manual used data from this report when constructing examples of benchmarks and graphs. The entire report is available via their Web site at: www.ci.portland.or.us/auditor.

Oregon Progress Board. *Oregon Benchmarks: Standards for Measuring Statewide Progress and Institutional Performance, Report to the 1995 Legislature.* **Salem, Oregon: Oregon Progress Board, December 1994.**

Describes the progress in the Oregon benchmarking project. Lists all 259 benchmarks and the state's progress in meeting those goals. A useful source for those of you who want to perform quality of life studies.

Willis, Alan. *American Suburbs Rating Guide and Fact Book: Ranks 1,770 Suburbs in 50 Metropolitan Areas.* **Milipatis, CA: Toucan Valley Publications, Inc., 1993.**

Ranks suburbs for the 50 largest metropolitan areas in the US. Rankings are based on such factors as economics, affordable housing, crime, open spaces and education. The text was used to provide an example of scorecarding.

Because of our total commitment to continuous improvement, we have provided our readers with a chance to give feedback.

Tear our this page and mail it to:

Community Benchmarks Program
102 Maxwell Hall
Syracuse, NY 13244-1090

Does this
Book ?
Measure Up

Or if you prefer...

Use the electronic feedback form on the Community Benchmarks Web Site:

www.maxwell.syr.edu/benchmarks

1. **How did you find out about this book?:**
   ❑ Web site (specify): _____
   ❑ Advertisement (note publication):_____ ❑ Colleague/Friend
   ❑ Direct Mail ❑ Professional or Accrediting Association: _____
   ❑ Other (please specify): _____

1. **Did this book meet your expectations?**   ❑ Yes   ❑ No   ❑ Not Sure
   Comments: _____
   _____
   _____

2. **If officials and citizens used the basic tools presented in this book, would local government and communities improve?**   ❑ Yes   ❑ No   ❑ Not Sure
   Comments: _____
   _____
   _____

3. **How would you improve this book?**
   _____
   _____
   _____

4. **If you would like us to respond to your comments, please indicate the best way to contact you.**
   _____
   _____

Thank you for your time.

Please use back of page for additional comments.